D0952214

More Praise for

LEADING FROM PURPOSE

"Finding my purpose has enabled me to tap into resilience I didn't even know I had. Leaders who have a clear purpose know what they stand for, what they do not stand for, and who they stand with, particularly during difficult times. *Leading from Purpose* is a must-read for all organizations that are interested in having leaders who can make fast, ethical decisions in times of change and ambiguity."

—*Selina Millstam, vice president and global head of Talent Management, Ericsson*

"Powerful things happen when people are connected to purpose. This book shows why and how. Nick Craig uses his wise insights and his well-honed gift of storytelling to teach and inspire us. *Leading from Purpose* is at once a road map and a revelation destined to become a classic in the purpose movement."

—*Richard Leider, author of* The Power of Purpose, Repacking Your Bags, *and* Life Reimagined

"How do you unleash the fullest potential of individuals and teams without knowing their super powers? The simple answer is that you can't. Nick Craig masters the balance of art and science in *Leading from Purpose*, effortlessly coaxing all of us to answer the biggest question of them all—why?"

—*Stacey Tank, vice president of corporate communications and external affairs, Home Depot*

"If you have been asking yourself the timeless question—'Am I truly living the meaningful life I was meant to lead?'—Craig's wisdom and understanding renders the answer crystal clear. For those in search of fulfillment, he guides you on a journey of self-discovery to realize your life's purpose so you may better lead."

—*Dana H. Born, PhD, U.S. air force brigadier general, ret., senior executive fellow at Harvard's Kennedy School of Government*

"Some say it takes up to 10,000 hours to master a skill. Fortunately, Nick Craig has done the hard work for us. I have been privileged to watch Craig up close as he has helped thousands of people discover their purpose over the past ten years. In this book, he shares with us those hard-won lessons of experience so that we too might find ourselves.... Craig is truly the Master of Purpose."

—*Scott A. Snook, senior lecturer of business administration, Harvard Business School*

"Nick Craig is on fire and the fire has driven him across the bridge of convention to the realm of sacred conversation and deep learning. In that realm, he has helped thousands to find their purpose, or unique gift. Now he returns with deeply synthesized insights. This book will turn the thousands into millions. If you want to know who you really are or what your organization is meant to do, this is a must-read."

—*Professor Robert E. Quinn, Center for Positive Organizations and University of Michigan*

LEADING
FROM
PURPOSE

Nick Craig

hachette
BOOKS

NEW YORK   BOSTON

Hachette Books

Hachette Book Group

1290 Avenue of the Americas

New York, NY 10104

hachettebookgroup.com

twitter.com/hachettebooks

First Edition: June 2018

Hachette Books is a division of Hachette Book Group, Inc.

The Hachette Books name and logo are trademarks of Hachette Book Group, Inc.

The publisher is not responsible for websites (or their content) that are not owned by the publisher.

The Hachette Speakers Bureau provides a wide range of authors for speaking events. To find out more, go to www.hachettespeakersbureau.com or call (866) 376-6591.

Icons made by Freepik from www.flaticon.

Library of Congress Control Number: 2018932907.

ISBNs: 978-0-316-41624-5 (hardcover), 978-0-316-41623-8 (ebook)

Printed in the United States of America

LSC-H

10 9 8 7 6 5 4 3 2 1

*To those who invested in little old me when it mattered
the most and saw what I couldn't see
Bill and Heide Craig (My parents!)
Hayden Porter
Ben Fordham
Bob Schaffer and Bob Neiman
Thomas Rice
Bob Quinn
Bill George
Scott Snook*

CONTENTS

CONTENTS

FOREWORD BY BRENÉ BROWN

I didn't know Nick Craig or his work when he approached me at a conference several years ago and said, "We should talk."

I had just finished delivering a three-hour workshop to 250 CEOs, and I was equal parts wiped out and pumped up. I stared at him for a few seconds, wondering *how* I could possibly segue his invitation-directive into a normal introduction, and right as I began to say, "I'm Brené. Nice to meet you," he said, "It was an incredible afternoon. Thank you. I know you're probably tired and energized—I want to talk about your amazing alchemist energy. And the tired part."

The rest of the conversation was weird and strangely compelling. He talked to me about his work and then offered to help me find my purpose. I didn't know why or what was happening at that moment, but I immediately said yes as I fought back tears. I rarely say yes.

A couple of years and many long conversations later, I offered to write the foreword for this book. But there was one condition. I told Nick that I wanted to frame it like a Surgeon General's warning. I thought he'd laugh but he said, "Yep. Makes total sense."

Here's the label I think the publisher should put on the outside of this book:

Caution: This is a book about purpose. Do this work and it will change the way you live, love, parent, and lead. However, you will not be able to forget, block, or unlearn your purpose, and trying to walk away from the reason you're here on this earth may cause anxiety, resentment, confusion, self-doubt, and persistent, low-grade feelings of "what in the hell am I doing?" Once you live your purpose, you can't unlive it.

Nick's purpose work isn't magic. It's the gift of clarity, focus, and confidence. I opened my heart and mind to my purpose work and, in turn, it's rearranged my life. My purpose is now the filter that I use to evaluate what work I do, and, more importantly, what I don't do. Do I live my purpose perfectly? No. Do I ever choose fear or scarcity over my purpose? Sometimes. But when I do, things fall apart. Including me at times.

I've spent my entire life wanting to be in service of something bigger. The most significant transformation for me has been learning (and relearning) that my most valuable contributions happen when I'm in my purpose.

And, I take back what I said about magic. Nick's work does provide clarity, focus, and confidence. And a little magic.

INTRODUCTION

In 2007, I stood before a group of senior leaders at a *Fortune* 50 company. I had been asked to teach a session on purpose as one of the modules in a two-day program on authentic leadership. At the time, even I thought that purpose's connection to leadership was questionable. After all, purpose was just one of 12 chapters in the fieldbook on authentic leadership that I had helped Bill George write a few years before.

Back then, I thought purpose was a poor cousin to other focus areas of leadership, such as knowing the crucible stories that shape us as leaders, clarifying our values, or leveraging our underutilized strengths. Those were the winners, so I emphasized them and spent less time with purpose.

Thus, when the firm asked me to include a module on purpose, I balked. They insisted, and with many reservations, I agreed. They were right, and I was wrong. And between 2007 and 2009, I had several opportunities to teach authentic leadership to the most challenging audience of leaders in a very challenging time in the company's history. The company's stock fell from 56 to 6. There could be no better litmus test of what was most useful to this group of leaders.

The way alumni described it, in the past, when extensive personnel cuts had become unavoidable or a dramatic change of direction had become necessary, there had always been an understanding that those who led through the difficult times and made the hard decisions would be taken care of. This time, however, things were different. The members of the top team faced dire circumstances on all fronts, and the only thing anyone knew for certain was that no one would be getting out unscathed. So, what do you do when your stock options have hit rock bottom, everyone's salary is questionable, and the entire future of the organization hangs in the balance?

Imagine what you would do.

One leader's answer stunned me. He said, "Look, I realized I didn't have any promises of stock options, bonuses, or promotions to help us anymore. All the external motivators I had depended on in the past were gone. The economic chaos we had all worried about was now at my dinner table. The only thing I could stand on was my *purpose as a leader* from the program. So, I told my team that I don't have anything to give them this time except for what I stand for, and my purpose is and always has been *to be the white-water raft guide who gets you safely to the other side*. If you don't want to do this I will understand, but if you stay we will go through the most challenging 12 months ever and I make no promises on the end game."

During that year this leader and his team did what they needed to do. They made many hard decisions that balanced investments in future growth with painful cuts in head count to keep the doors open. At the time, although the business was starting to show positive numbers, the big success was that he still had the same team and they were more trusting and connected than any team he had ever worked with before.

As a well-trained cynic, I figured I was looking at a 1-in-1,000 occurrence. It turned out I was looking at a 1-in-10 occurrence, and that was during a period in which we spent very little time on purpose in the program.

Fast-forward to 2009. Paul Polman had just taken over as CEO of Unilever, then a $40 billion consumer products company competing with Procter & Gamble and Nestlé. Polman put forth a bold vision of revenue growth while dramatically reducing the firm's environmental footprint over 10 years—this for an organization that made everything from salad dressing to laundry detergent.

We were asked to run the leadership transformation program for the top 1,200 leaders. Once again, purpose was one of eight topics. However, in an environment in which each leader had to find a way to do what had never been attempted before, purpose became the element that made the impossible possible. The typically mundane process of creating individual leadership development plans was transformed when each one got reviewed by the CEO and top executives; there, in bold letters, was the leader's purpose.

Eighteen to 24 months later, as alumni returned to the program, their stories and the impact of purpose once again surprised me. They defined their goals and approached issues in new and different ways, clearly affected by their purpose. Leaders were promoted to positions they would have never gotten before, or decided to stay in a job and do it right as opposed to climbing the proverbial ladder. They had authentic conversations with their bosses about what needed to be done to turn the business around. All this happened just because of a set of words that for them captured their "purpose." One leader said, "You know, given my purpose, what is clear for me is if things really aren't challenging I get bored and when I get bored I don't live my purpose. Growing the region by 15 percent over three years is boring. Now, *doubling* the business—that's a challenge, and that's what I am going to do, and here is how we will do it." Truth be told, he didn't double it, but he reached way above 15 percent, and the changes he made in the business, as well as the way in which he led, created a very different arc than he would have traced if he had not known his purpose.

Seeing story after story like this forced me to realize that something was happening with purpose that was different from all the other beautiful parts of authentic leadership. Purpose isn't "one of 12 elements." Purpose is the stage on which all the other elements (values, strengths, self-awareness, etc.) create great leadership. If leadership were on stage, purpose is what gives you Broadway and London's Globe Theater. Without it, you get your local production of *King Lear*.

Leading from purpose for real people

Since 2009, we have taken our work on purpose and authentic leadership (how you live your purpose) around the world to retailers in Australia, oil and gas engineers in Oklahoma, engineering and scientific organizations in Boston, pharmaceutical companies in Sweden, West Point faculty, and many more leaders and organizations. Each time, I've looked out at the audience of intimidating, world-class senior leaders and said to myself,

"This will be the place where purpose is the wrong shoe on the wrong foot." I have been positively surprised every time.

If you are reading this and thinking, "But I am not a leader," then think again. If you make decisions that affect others in any part of your life, then you're leading—even if your current story is something different. You can lead *without* clarity of purpose or *with* it . . . which is it going to be?

This book is written from the gritty realities of senior executives who make everything from peanut butter to special pumps for oil and gas exploration. In it you will find a down-to-earth and accessible orientation to purpose and how it can have a significant impact on leading in the twenty-first century—not to mention compelling stories of what has happened as executives have stepped into living their purpose.

Great causes such as ending poverty and injustice are wonderful ways to express purpose, but real leaders need to align themselves with something that works just as well for managing unruly customers, competitors that won't sit still, and global events that turn strategy into dust. Sounds more like your world? Most of our lives include interacting with family and friends, getting paid a fair price for what we do, raising kids, getting laid off, hiring people we find out can't walk the talk, giving someone a break when nobody else will, and the list goes on. These are the places where purpose helps us the most. Most of what is "sold" as purpose does us all a great disservice by making us feel that we are less than those who "have it" and that we must either be bathed in light or give up trying. Nothing could be further from the truth.

What if you were already full of purpose but you didn't know it? Good news! You are and always will be. You can and *will* run away from your purpose, but for most of us it is always there, waiting for us to remember and invite it back in. We just need to slow down long enough for it to be found. It's the only thing that will never reject you, judge you, dump you, or betray you, even though we will do all those things to *it* in the process of coming to truly own the one thing that defines our unique gift in this lifetime. My hope is that as you read the stories and examples based on over 100 in-depth interviews of leaders from every walk of life, you will begin to see what has been unseen in your journey as a leader: the purpose that is yours.

Leading is about translating what is possible into reality. Whether you know it or not, you already serve others in a unique way that changes your reality and that of others. You may be thinking, "Now that's a stretch. I have no clue what my purpose *is*, so why talk about living it?" The good news is that by discovering how you are already living it, you will be able to "see" it.

Over the last 10 years, we have worked with more than 10,000 senior executives to help them discover and have the courage to *live* their purpose. For 95 percent of them it wasn't about quitting their job and going to work for Save the Children, or leaving their spouse, or telling their boss to stuff it; it was about realizing that purpose is present in every moment, and we can choose to operate from it or *not*. It's evident in how we interact with the challenges of the moment, not in what role, title, or office we have.

Purpose will make you feel curious, courageous, humbled,

and inspired, as well as vulnerable, scared, confused, and much more…but with purpose, it all has meaning; without it, sometimes life is great and other times it's not.

I think that you'll enjoy reading the many stories of people who have led from purpose. Most of them are not famous people or CEOs; rather, these individuals are from all levels, of all ages, and from every part of the globe. Each was willing to spend hours being interviewed. The leaders whose stories ended up in this book spent even more time with me, refining our insights and going deeper into the truth of what it means to lead from purpose. I had not talked to or seen many of the people I interviewed for 5 or 10 years, so each interview was a journey of discovery for both of us.

How this book is structured

By seeing how others have traveled, you, too, will have a better sense of your purpose and what leading from purpose can represent. More importantly, you will be able to step more fully each day into living it and leading others on the journey with you.

Part One of this book focuses on what purpose is and why it's important. It describes three pathways we have found that help us see how it "leads" us, and shares many examples of what others have found. Note that although we communicate our purpose through language and a set of words that we call our *purpose statement*, the reality is that the statement is just words and our purpose is much more than words. The words are like a key that unlocks a door. The key by itself, like a purpose statement, has no value. It's the room that we access because of the key that matters, the purpose that has always been leading us. We have found three powerful means of not only discovering the key but, more importantly, stepping into the room of purpose:

- Magical moments, from childhood to early adulthood
- The most challenging experiences in our life—our crucibles
- A passion that has fueled us over time

Part Two guides you to finding your own purpose. By looking at some examples of authentic purpose statements and working through some simple exercises, you will be able to identify—or at least come close to—your own purpose statement. You may want to do this before reading about the impact of purpose in the lives of real leaders, or you may want to simply skim this section and return to it later.

Finally, Part Three drills down on the reality of what it's like to lead from purpose. This isn't a Disney story; let this be a warning to those who are looking for purpose to magically make all your problems go away. You need to go to some other book if that's what you are looking for. The world of real purpose is much more confronting, compelling, and in the end satisfying than any quick fix. You will be stretched and tested in so many ways that, if having it easy is your goal, you should take a pass on purpose.

But the result will be worth the effort. A life lit by purpose is one of clarity and meaning. You don't need purpose when things are going well, but when the tough decisions must be made, purpose points to the answer. Most important, others will want to follow you when purpose is leading you, and you are leading from your purpose.

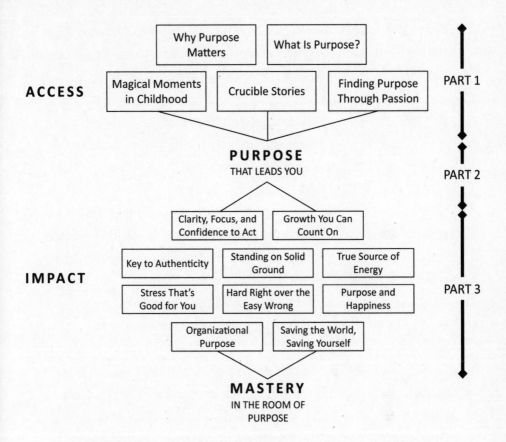

Leading from Purpose self-assessment

Before taking you through your purpose-driven leadership journey, I welcome you to take the Leading from Purpose Self-Assessment at www.coreleader.com/survey. At the end of the book I will encourage you to take it again, and see the impact of purpose.

PART I →

ACCESS

Chapter 1

WHY PURPOSE MATTERS

To be nobody but yourself in a world which is doing its best, night and day, to make you everybody else means to fight the hardest battle which any human being can fight; and never stop fighting.

—e. e. cummings

Are you willing to be led by someone who is not clear about their purpose? What if that person is you?

Mind you, I'm not talking about an *objective*. You can probably rattle off your objectives in two seconds. But do you have clarity about what purpose is leading you? If you've gotten this far, something must be working. So, wouldn't it be nice if you had a clear idea of what that is? Face it: If you don't know it, you can't fully live it. And if you aren't living it, you can't lead from it.

It's worth figuring it out. When you get clarity of purpose, you see the world through a unique filter, and this gives you the opportunity to be much more creative and innovative about how you lead in your life. It creates "meaning" from events and actions that, over time, shape your impact on the world. If you study the people you admire most in history, the ones who had the most impact—whether it's Eleanor Roosevelt, John Kennedy,

Nelson Mandela, or Steve Jobs—you'll notice that each operated from a very different view of the world compared to those around them, and then they got the world to see things their way.

You are more than your role

William Shakespeare reminds us of what our lives will consist of when we lack clarity of purpose. According to these well-known lines from *As You Like It*, we are all actors in a play.

> *All the world's a stage,*
> *and all the men and women merely players,*
> *They have their exits and entrances,*
> *And one man in his time plays many parts,*
> *His acts being seven ages.*

Today our seven ages move from school days through college and graduate school, to the wisdom of senior roles, to retirement and inevitable death. The modern version of this play includes frequent flyer miles, stock options, and the possibility of staying on people's cell-phone "Favorites" list long after we are gone. No matter what costumes we wear, Shakespeare shows us what the unexamined life looks like, the journey without purpose.

The challenge for many of us is that our identity and sense of self are based on our role, title, profession, house, or car, which are all fleeting and fragile by nature.

I have spent most of the last 10 years with people who have the big jobs. The problem is, many feel lost, struggling, with a sense of misplaced identity. They can't say it because everyone else is congratulating them on their success. What they loved wasn't the title or the job; it was the work they did and the impact they made. The more we see the impact of our work on others, the more meaning we get from it. The higher we go, the farther away we find ourselves from the people and things we impact.

Thus, clarity of meaning from within becomes even more important. No one can take your purpose away from you; it is your real identity. Purpose has deep resilience and staying power in a way that nothing else can or will. Who are you beyond what you do? Purpose helps us answer this question. Purpose is the deep well that always has water.

We are brought up in the context of our childhood, culture, and education; much of who we are is the result of our circumstances. All the events that happen around us shape us. But, eventually, we must ask ourselves: What is steering us on this journey as we go through life?

This book is filled with the stories of people who have rediscovered the purpose that is leading them and the impact that is the outcome of this discovery. Here is an excellent example of someone who used his purpose to step out of the script that had been handed to him.

Jostein Solheim, CEO of Ben & Jerry's, was regarded as a high-potential leader at Unilever (corporate owner of Ben & Jerry's). He grew up in the ice cream business and was the fix-it guy, the one you go to when a turnaround is needed. Because of this, he quickly rose through the management ranks. By the time he reached the top job at Ben & Jerry's, he had worked in over 30 countries and moved more times than he could remember. "Get it, fix it, and move on" was his modus operandi. After only 18 months at Ben &

Jerry's, he had taken a business that was in single-digit decline and turned it into double-digit growth. The iconic brand that everyone loved was back in the game and winning.

Now he was being groomed for the big prize of senior vice president of ice cream, overseeing operations in multiple countries—the one he had spent his whole career preparing for, the final ascension to the top ranks of a multibillion-dollar consumer goods company. Here he would get the significant raise, stock options, and global title, a role that defines success.

Only one thing stood in his way: his purpose. Timing is everything in life, and now that he was about to jump, he got the chance to clarify his purpose:

> **JOSTEIN—Helping people thrive in paradox and ambiguity for things that really matter.**

Remember that the purpose statement is just a set of words. Yet these words are like a key to unlock a door to the room of purpose that leads each of us. For Jostein, his room of purpose revealed an important dilemma. The promotion would put him beyond doing work that *really* mattered and into managing others who would. In all his jobs, Jostein had saved people's jobs, enabled groups to do things they didn't believe they could do, and developed those reporting to him who otherwise would have been left behind. He was happiest when all hell was breaking loose with no end in sight. Whether sailing in a storm or fixing a business that everyone thought was broken, Jostein was your man. Now he had found a stage to live his purpose, but it didn't fit with the current plan.

Purpose doesn't wait or care about the plan, it whispers in

our ear and says...*follow me.* Leading isn't about going where everyone else is going, it's about creating something that didn't previously exist.

Jostein was used to creating five-year strategic plans solely as a means of funding his next year's budget. Now his purpose was asking for much more: Stay for a long time and do something that matters. Ben & Jerry's had a social agenda that was like no other. Climate change, fair trade, and non-GMO sourcing were all ideas that needed leading. If he stayed, they might really take off, and if he left they might falter as the new CEO spent 12 months just getting up to speed. Here was an opportunity to do something that really mattered.

Many of us have stood in Jostein's shoes—do you follow your heart or your head? As my colleague Bill George so eloquently says, "The greatest distance we will ever travel is between our head and heart."

Listening to his purpose, Jostein did the one thing that no one expected. He turned down the six-figure raise, stock options, and everything else that went with the promotion and decided to stay at Ben & Jerry's. Not only did he decide to stay, he bought a house for the first time in his life, having moved every two years up until then. He was all-in.

According to Jostein, creating a five-year strategy when you know you will be in charge throughout all five years is very different from drafting something that gets you what you need now that others will fix later. Jostein doesn't take all the credit for Ben & Jerry's success; he is the first to say that he is just an enabler for the magical work that others do. But, had he not been the steady hand that stayed seven-plus years, there is a long list of things we probably wouldn't have seen from Ben & Jerry's, among them the following:

- Double-digit growth each year in a declining overall market
- 100 percent fair trade sourcing
- 100 percent non-GMO sourcing

Ben & Jerry's also embraced climate justice advocacy, including endorsing carbon pricing that works and lobbying political leaders to support United Nations climate change initiatives. Jostein was even hugged by Al Gore at the United Nations Paris climate change meeting.

Jostein could have taken the big promotion and continued his success at Unilever's corporate headquarters. Or he could have moved home to Europe and found another opportunity. Purpose is most valuable to us when there are no right answers, just choices for which time alone will give us the clarity to choose wisely. The gift of operating from purpose is that we know what to do. The challenge is that we know, and the world may not be happy with us as a result. In Jostein's case, his success two or three years down the road made the decision to stay look easy in hindsight. At the time, however, his bosses, his wife, and his kids didn't see his decision as the right one. You know you're in the world of purpose when you have sleepless nights and challenging discussions that don't have easy answers, and you've got to do it anyway.

In the moments in which we must make the hardest choices in our life, do we follow the advice of others or the voice within? The challenge for most of us is we don't have a clear inner voice that we trust. We have multiple voices in our heads and they rarely sing in harmony. If you don't know it, you can't live it. And if you aren't living it, you can't lead from it.

Why is purpose so important now?

Purpose isn't a new idea. In the second century, Roman Emperor Marcus Aurelius wrote his "Meditations." His reflections on life, leadership, and dealing with bureaucracy and hypocrisy are ageless, as are his thoughts on the importance of purpose: *"Everything came into being for a purpose and is drawn toward the achievement of its purpose."* Yet, even though it's a very old idea, most of our parents never talked about their purpose. They talked about their desires, dreams, aspirations, and accomplishments, but rarely about purpose. So why should we pay any more attention to purpose than our parents or anybody else since Marcus Aurelius's times?

One reason is that there is so much recent research and information demonstrating the power of purpose. Over the past five years, there has been an explosion of interest in purpose in the business world. Harvard Business School's head of strategy, Cynthia Montgomery, has eloquently argued that a leader's most important role is to be a steward of his or her organization's purpose. Martin Seligman, the father of positive psychology, has described purpose as the pathway to flourishing. Daniel Pink, in his book *Drive*, which summarizes 50 years of research on what motivates us in the workplace, identifies purpose as one of three keys to exceptional performance in the twenty-first century (autonomy and opportunity for mastery are the other two). Research on women leaders by Herminia Ibarra concludes that clarity of purpose is essential to holding on to your identity as the world tries to turn you into one of the boys.

Purpose is equally important at the organizational level. *Harvard Business Review* and the Energy Project gathered data from 20,000 employees across 25 industries on how they feel at work and how they perform as a result. The presence or lack of purpose turned out to have the highest single impact.

But more importantly, purpose-driven leaders had an especially powerful impact on their employees. Those leaders whom employees felt had clarity of purpose and communicated it inspired their employees to be:

Employees who derive meaning from their work:

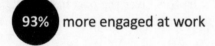 more likely to stay with their organizations

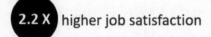 higher job satisfaction

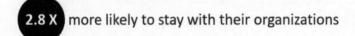 more engaged at work

Yet the same report indicated that fewer than 20 percent of leaders could communicate any purpose or direction that had meaning.

Another study, by the DeVry University Career Advisory Board, looked at millennials' attitudes regarding employment issues. They found that 71 percent of millennials ranked finding meaningful work as one of the top three key elements they used to evaluate their career success, and 30 percent of millennials reported it as the single most important element. The bottom line being that millennials are willing to sacrifice more traditional career comforts—standard work hours, competitive pay—in pursuit of more meaningful work.

On the personal side, almost every month more studies appear on the abundant benefits of having clarity of purpose. Most of these studies leverage the Ryff scales of Psychological Well-Being, which have been validated as an effective measure of one's level of life purpose. Using these scales with study populations in the thousands over 3- to 10-year periods has allowed the results to be definitive. It appears that there is probably nothing you could do that would help you live a longer and healthier life than to be clear on your purpose and to lead from it.

These studies have highlighted many benefits accruing to people with a strong sense of purpose.

Leaders whom employees felt had clarity of purpose and communicated it inspired their employees to be:

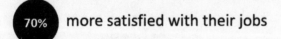 **more satisfied with their jobs**

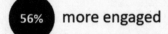 **more engaged**

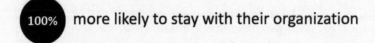 **more likely to stay with their organization**

As compelling as the data is, it is still about as motivating as eating well, exercising, getting eight hours of sleep, and the long list of other things we would do if we had time. Until we realize that the real driver for purpose is something much more urgent.

Emergence of the VUCA world

How do you lead in a world in which the ground is shifting under your feet and all the rules are changing as you play the game? This is the situation most of us wake up to every day. What industry or organization won't go through more change in the next 5 years than it has in the last 50? From taxis to hotels, to oil and gas, banking, retail, publishing—all industries are in flux or struggling.

The roots of this new urgency around purpose can be found in the 1990s. The 1991 collapse of the Soviet Union was a seismic change for the U.S. military. Who would we fight and what would it look like, given that everything we had prepared for was gone? To codify this emerging context, the U.S. military created the concept of "VUCA"—volatile, uncertain, complex/chaotic, and ambiguous—and used it to address the challenges facing leaders in this new world.

From leadership in a world that was:	To leadership in a world that is VUCA:
Rational	**Volatile:** Change happens rapidly and on a large scale.
Predictable	**Uncertain:** The future can't be predicted with any precision.
Simple	**Complex and Chaotic:** There are few single causes or solutions. Solutions emerge from within the system as opposed to being imposed from outside. Change is continuous, with few predictable markers.
Linear	**Ambiguous:** Little clarity on what events mean and their effect. "Info" is incomplete or indecipherable.

New and lopsided demographics are accelerating the changes: According to the United Nations Population Fund, for the first time in history a quarter of humanity is between the ages of 12 and 24. India alone has almost the same number of 15- to 34-year-olds as the combined populations of the United States, Canada, and Britain. The downstream implications are mind-boggling: many of the institutions and societal promises we take for granted will require completely different solutions or face collapse.

In the pre-VUCA days, the solution was to define a vision and strategy, and then align all the resources to execute "the plan." We worked in two- to five-year time frames and everyone complained bitterly when external events forced a strategy change. Today, any strategic plan that lasts longer than a yearly budget cycle is impressive. We all understand why strategic plans are continually being redone. Yet, we all want a level of certainty and guidance on how to build something over time that matters.

What do you lead from, when what used to be strategic is now tactical, and what is tactical happens on your smartphone? In uncharted territories with no reliable landmarks, people and organizations need a compass to guide them. Purpose has become the new compass. It defines the "why" and, in many cases, the unique "how" by which leaders and organizations do their work. One benefit of purpose is that it doesn't change—as opposed to strategy, which these days is always changing, morphing, and being turned inside out.

Purpose has always been important. The data is compelling as to the value of purpose not only in our work but also in our life overall. In today's VUCA world, without purpose there is little to stand on that will survive. Millennials value it much more highly than other generations, and for good reason. Let's ask the question one more time: Are you willing to be led by someone who is not clear about his or her purpose?

Before we move to uncovering the path to finding purpose, I want to bring home just how powerful one's purpose can be. When we interview leaders in our programs, one of our key questions is, "What happens to your purpose when you are in a highly stressful situation?" Guess what Jostein Solheim's answer to this question was: Mr. Thrives-in-paradox-and-ambiguity is at his *most* calm and centered when all hell breaks loose.

Jostein loves sailing and lives on Lake Champlain near Burlington, Vermont. In the winter the lake freezes over so solidly you can drive on it; therefore, sailing in May is a brisk adventure in which being in the water for any length of time is dangerous. Jostein's son Jachov took a dingy sailboat out and hit a log, losing the rudder. Jachov jumped in the water and tried to swim to shore, but the wind blew him farther out. Through his binoculars, Jostein could see the sailboat—with no sail and no Jochav. With no other boats in the water this early in the season, Jostein dialed 911; it took the Coast Guard 30 minutes to find Jachov, hanging on to a buoy with borderline hypothermia. Jostein's wife and friends were freaking out during this adventure, but Jostein was as calm and clearheaded as could be. He worked with the Coast Guard to get his son, retrieved the boat, and said goodbye to his friends. Then, and only then, did he get the shakes.

The beauty of purpose is that it truly has us. We don't *find* our purpose; more, we reconnect to and can consciously lead from it. Whether Jostein is running a meeting or dealing with his son in the water, he leads from his purpose and thrives in ambiguity and paradox for things that matter. Put him in a stable and steady environment and he will be distracted and ineffective. Put him in the VUCA world and he is your man.

Now, let's dive deeper into what purpose really is.

Points to ponder

1. What is it about the topic of purpose that intrigues you?
2. How do you make sure you don't just end up with lots of frequent flyer miles in the end?
3. Where do you lead from within yourself?
4. Have you ever made a decision like Jostein's, that went against everyone else's view and in the end turned out to be the best decision?
5. Would you radically change the strategic plan for your business unit or organization if you knew with certainty that you would be present for the next five years?
6. What is the version of the VUCA world that you experience in your organization? How do you find solid ground?

Chapter 2

WHAT IS PURPOSE?

Everyone is a genius...but if you judge a fish by its ability to climb a tree, it will live its whole life believing that it is stupid.

This quotation is popularly attributed to Albert Einstein. It shines a spotlight on the gift of leading from one's purpose. Until we know our purpose, we don't know if we are a fish or a bobcat; when someone asks us to climb a tree, we attempt to do so. Over the course of our career, others assess us, coach and mentor us, and give us performance reviews in the belief that we can become closer to what they define as "perfection." When tree climbing doesn't work, we may feel humiliated, and yet the basic design of the process guarantees that we will feel a little stupid in the end.

Before I knew the purpose that was leading me, I spent my time trying to be a better version of what everyone wanted me to be. I had no problem going to meetings and providing input and hopefully some value. I realized that I wasn't really leading my team, rather just polishing what they had done. Pushing myself up a level via my purpose and what I can do has been a huge unlock. I realized my focus needed to be on "What can I uniquely do within my organization?" Do that first. Don't just polish everyone else's stuff. It has made me a more congruent leader even when I have to do what I don't want to do. Too much of the time, I have watched myself and others act based on what we thought we were supposed to do, while Rome burns. Purpose has helped me see that this is not what I am paid for. My purpose allows me to unlock that which nobody else can do.

—*Peter S., SVP Marketing*

You might say that Peter has stopped climbing the tree and started swimming.

Purpose: Your unique gift

After working with thousands of leaders over the last 10 years—underneath all the statements, experiences, insights, *aha!*s, and impacts, one common thread has emerged as the core essence of what purpose is and what it is not.

Purpose was present when you were a kid and will still be the same when you are 102. It's the essence of who you are and what you can bring to a situation that is "you." It has been leading you all your life; you just don't know it. You have only one purpose, yet it has many different expressions across the different aspects of your life.

I used to have a real problem with the word *purpose*. A lot of ink has been spilled on the topic over the past 15 years, and most authors seem to assume that everyone has a clear idea of what it is. Unfortunately, the dozens of definitions and "five easy steps" exercises to finding it usually end up making people feel *worse*, not better, and leave them no closer to understanding their own purpose than they were when they started.

Think of it this way. Let's say we replaced you with someone equal to you in skill and mastery in your job and key roles in life. In three months, we interviewed all the people you used to interact with and asked them, "What do you miss most?" Their answer to that question tells you your purpose: the thing you bring to the table that disappears if you don't show up. Unfortunately, because we have spent our lives chasing after everyone's expectations of who we should be, we never know the one thing that makes the biggest difference, the purpose that has been leading us all our life.

The words *unique gift* are important whenever we speak about purpose. Purpose acts as a unique lens through which each of us sees the world. Looking through our own lens, each of us sees possibilities or does something that others would not have seen or done. That difference is a source of innovation and impact to which we all aspire. We don't produce innovation by copying someone else. We all know of leaders and innovators whose lens of purpose allowed them to see possibilities to which others were oblivious. Xerox's PARC lab in Palo Alto, California, was sitting on a prototype "mouse," a user-friendly interface, and connectivity—key technologies that could have enabled a revolution in personal computing before Steve Jobs and his team paid a visit in 1979. PARC personnel failed to see what Jobs—who aspired to use technology to change the world—was prepared to see. For most of us, it's subtler than this—it's how we tell a story, give feedback to someone who has screwed up, write a blog, close down a factory, or deliver a big presentation to a thousand employees.

What do you see that others cannot because of the purpose that propels you? Do you know what that purpose is?

Let's unpack the rest of the sentence: "Purpose is the unique gift *that you bring to the world*."

No one lives their purpose in a vacuum. Our purpose only shows itself to us when we express it in the world around us— just as a movie isn't really a movie until it's shown on a screen. I am not convinced that "making the world a better place" or "serving others" is necessary for purpose to be alive. I do know that it's the dance between our purpose and the purposes of others that allows us to witness and experience how purpose leads us. The real benefit of purpose shows itself when it leads us in our life.

Peeling back the layers of purpose

There are many definitions of purpose out there and many of them are wonderful expressions of *how* we might lead from our purpose.

One I hear goes as follows: "You love it; you are very good at it; you are paid well for it; and the world needs it." But I have found that our purpose is just as likely to be in evidence when all those conditions are *not* true. If we must wait until everything is working before we live and lead from our purpose, then most of us will have a long wait. The people we deeply admire, the ones who have made an impact on the world, didn't have this kind of smooth sailing, and public acclaim wasn't their motivation. In fact, many of the leaders I have worked with could check all these boxes but still didn't know their purpose. Finding their purpose had a significant impact on how they led from that moment onward; we will hear many of their stories over the course of this book.

People who lead from purpose stick with it when no one is supporting them, and they do it anyway. What if the real criterion for leading from your purpose was "you can't help but do it; you are not good at it (compared to what the world asks you to do); nobody will pay you to do it; and you wonder if you really have lost your mind"?

"A cause larger and more enduring than ourselves" is commonly associated with purpose. A compelling cause is a powerful strategy by which we express our purpose. With luck, you will be passionate about several causes, careers, and adventures in your life. Unfortunately, many of the leaders I have worked with who are committed to a cause also admit they feel exhausted, physically and emotionally. I recently worked with a chief sustainability officer who was suffering from burnout. The "cause" was creating sustainability in a very large global corporation. How does it make sense to be the leader of sustainability while not being sustainable? Wouldn't sustainability start with herself? It was only when we clarified how she could lead from her purpose that we were able to unlock a path forward that made sense. Thus, a cause is a great thing and it's a wonderful *vehicle* through which many people live their purpose, but it's *not* your purpose.

Aspirational purpose—another common approach—yields

a purpose that may not be the core essence of who we are; rather, it is who we want to become. "To be the bright shining star of possibility" is great if that is what you operate from when the worst happens to you. But if it's what you want your purpose to be because you are running away from your real purpose, you are fooling yourself. If your purpose is "To be the restless explorer of the liberating truth," life isn't always going to be a party, yet you have the opportunity to have a powerful impact in the world. You have a gift; the question is, are you willing to fully own it?

Your purpose is more than the sum of your values. From the Apostle Paul to Mother Teresa, there are more than 800 saints in the Christian faith. Most of these saints shared the same values, yet they were beautifully different in their expression of their values and faith. Each had a purpose that determined how they brought their unique gift to this world. According to Mary Gentile in her groundbreaking book *Giving Voice to Values*, there are five values that people around the globe share:

- Honesty
- Respect
- Responsibility
- Fairness
- Compassion

It's easy to know the list; the hard part is living by them in challenging situations that we have not experienced before. Gentile works with students all over the world to practice living their values, using very powerful and difficult case studies that mimic the real world. There is no one way to do it right; rather, each of us has the opportunity to live our values in our own unique way. Our purpose crafts our expression of our values.

Finally, and perhaps most important in the leadership context, purpose is more than a combination of your divisional goals and personal KPIs (key performance indicators). Thus, "Increase sales in my region by 12 percent while fostering teamwork and staff development" may define the goals that are an expression of your purpose, yet the core essence of who you are is much deeper. Nor is your purpose an encapsulation of your accomplishments, no matter how impressive. I remember one program participant who introduced himself as "Tom, the inventor of [a well-known drug used by millions]." Many of us define ourselves by the expertise or thing the world values about us. But *if you can be fired from it or retire from it, it's not your purpose*. Each of these are a wonderful expression of the purpose that is leading us:

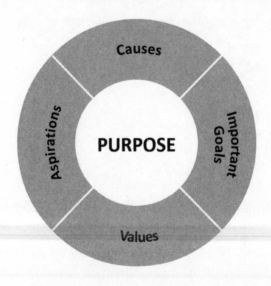

The benefit of defining purpose as the unique gift you bring to the world

You may be saying, knowing my unique gift is no more helpful than "Do what you love and follow your passions." The two aren't at all equivalent. Your unique gift is deeper, immutable. Our passions change; so does what we love (many of us have divorced that person). Purpose may become more refined and more developed over time, but its underlying thread stays the same. That unique gift that you bring, your purpose, will:

1. Bring meaning to life's challenges
2. Endure through your entire life
3. Work no matter what you "do"
4. Work in all parts of your life
5. Relieve the "imposter syndrome"
6. Bring out the curious little child that is still inside of you

Let's consider each of those in turn.

1. Purpose brings meaning to life's challenges.

Our world is no longer (if it ever was) predictable or simple. One of the most critical measures of your ability to lead others in any environment is how you respond when something unpleasant happens that affects you and the people you work with: the appearance of a competitor's game-changing product, a major client's defection, a recession, or a catastrophe such as 9/11.

People will ask, "What does this mean?" How you answer that question will set the story people will tell themselves and influence the actions they will take.

Purpose is the creator of meaning; it is, at its core, a meaning machine. It is the filter through which we see the world.

Thomas Jefferson wrote the Declaration of Independence, clearly stating the purpose of a new nation in the document.

> We hold these truths to be self-evident, that all men are created equal, that they are endowed by their Creator with certain unalienable Rights, that among these are Life, Liberty and the pursuit of Happiness.

These words, possibly some of the best-known in the English language, sum up the purpose leading Jefferson and the Founding Fathers. During the American Civil War, Lincoln saw these words as the moral standard the nation should strive toward. The meaning he attributed to them was a driving element in his decision to draft the Emancipation Proclamation ending slavery in the United States.

When people rediscover their purpose, they often see how the events that have occurred throughout their life make sense in a way that they hadn't seen before. The world they are leading in looks different because they now clearly know what their unique gift brings to the picture. The Declaration of Independence defines the unique gift of what it means to be an American. For each of us, our personal purpose has as much meaning as Jefferson's words have for the United States.

2. Your purpose will endure through your entire life.

Your purpose today will ring as true when you are 102 as it does today. Purpose is the one thing that doesn't change when all else does—your job, circumstances, short-term goals. If your purpose changes with circumstances and the weather, it is not your true purpose. Though the VUCA world regularly topples our plans, true purpose persists, transcending business success and failure, illness, mergers, being fired, and taking on new jobs. The words you use to express your purpose may change, but its core essence does not. What's left after we are gone from this earth? The longer we are gone, the less day-to-day things will be remembered and the more the unique thing that we alone brought to the world, our purpose, remains.

3. Purpose works no matter what you "do."

When you connect with your purpose, it immediately applies to what you are doing; there is no need to change jobs or move to India to feed the poor. Many of the things we do, do *not* involve ending world poverty, hunger, war, or cancer. Purpose should be available in every context. We can't wait for some altruistic organization to call us up and say, "You have just won a trip to a meaningful purpose." Some of the most unhappy and purposeless people I have met have worked for what others perceived to be the most "purposeful" organizations. Some of the most purposeful leaders I have met do the most uncompelling things, like sell deodorant.

Purpose shows itself in how we interact with the challenges of the moment, not what role, title, or office we have. It is with us every day and we can choose to live from it at any moment. How we express it in the world over time is the outcome of many strategies, tactics, and lucky breaks.

4. Purpose works in all parts of your life.

I have seen leaders who believe their purpose is to transform their business, and the outcome is a family that is profoundly *not* transformed and a business leader who is alone and divorced. Settling for a surface-level purpose, or confusing *purpose* with *cause*, can create that "cobbler's children have no shoes" dilemma. The fallacy of thinking our purpose applies only to our work life becomes glaringly obvious when we tell our family members, "I have a purpose, but it has nothing to do with you." On the contrary, when you discuss your purpose with your friends and spouse—not just the people who pay you—they should say, "Yes! That is really *you*."

Most people start by "directing" their purpose externally—it's certainly easier—but purpose doesn't fully enter our lives until we can apply it to ourselves as well as to everyone else. This is usually the last step, and we experience its true value *only* when we apply it to ourselves and our personal lives. Our purpose may nudge us to create an untraditional family life, defining who does what and how we spend our time together in surprising ways, but it doesn't create a partitioned world in which "I live my purpose in my work, but I am a loser at home." Our purpose is present in all parts of our lives. Simply put, if you can't apply your purpose to yourself, it's not your purpose.

5. Purpose relieves the "imposter syndrome."

The world has no end of expectations and demands on who we should be. This can make us anxious and fearful. About 40 percent of the leaders I have met—even successful ones—suffer from "imposter syndrome." They think that everyone else deserves to be in the room, but not them. They wonder, "When will people figure out that I'm not up to the job?" That affliction goes away when you discover and begin living your purpose. Purpose produces compatibility among the different and often conflicting parts of your persona, allowing you to truly "be" your authentic self. It is that authenticity that earns respect and induces others to follow. If you don't know it, you can't lead from it, and if you can't lead from it, who are you following?

6. The curious young child inside of you will show up.

If your purpose makes you serious and dull, it's not your purpose. If there is one single trait of leading from the depth of your purpose, it is this: When the curious young child inside of you is smiling, you are in the room of purpose. This is where all the energy, aliveness, curiosity, insight, and full engagement are generated. Let's be clear, I am not talking about the actual kid that you might have been growing up. For some of us, those times were tough. I am talking about the curious youngster that is inside every one of us no matter what our journey has been.

To be truly useful, a purpose needs to pass some stringent tests. None of the following common definitions meets those tests.

- **A cause**. Saving whales and ending hunger are fine expressions of purpose, but they exclude many aspects of your life.
- **Your role, job, or occupation**. These describe what you do. If an equally capable person took your role, the quality people would say they miss about you is your purpose—not what you did, but how you did it.
- **Aspirations of great success**. Becoming the next Adele or major league baseball player may be fantastic expressions of your purpose, but they will not pass the test of time.

What we are left with is the core essence of who you are, the unique gift that you bring the world. What we have most in our control is the unique meaning we make of the moments in our life.

Thus, we end where we started. The events in our lives are just that: simply events. Yet we each have a story about what they mean. We only need to look at the data about eyewitness reports to glimpse how differently two people will retell the same event. We are the meaning makers of our journey in life. Purpose will create a significant alignment and clarity of the events in your life. Things that didn't make sense or fit will fall into place, and the overall compelling "story" becomes clear. You see what has been leading you, your purpose. Once you own that, you can lead from it. As this book will show you, it will have a profound impact on how you lead and who you are as a leader.

By now, I hope you are convinced of the value of reconnecting with your purpose and finding a way to lead from it, both at work and in your personal life. You've probably given some thought to what your own purpose might be, and maybe come up with a phrase or two to describe it. Maybe you're partway there, but you know in your heart that it doesn't open the door to your purpose.

The process itself is predictable. In fact, the same scene unfolds as each person in our program discovers his or her purpose. When it's over, the person who appeared disengaged has become fully animated, engaged, dynamic, and powerful. It is as if someone had switched on the electricity. Everyone around can feel the change as the individual emerges with a clear sense of his or her purpose and a plan for applying it.

So, where should one begin? Books that aim to help people discover what is important to them often suggest the following as a starting point: Write down what you would want included in your eulogy, or in toasts offered at your eightieth birthday. Alternatively, describe what you would do if you had all the money and time in the world. Surely, these books argue, this would reveal the deeper purpose that drives you. Unfortunately, these exercises produce stock answers that reveal very little. For example, when asked what they would do with sudden wealth, most people say the same thing: "I'd travel the world and then set up a charitable foundation." Instead, as research on lottery winners has shown, only a small percentage of them use their newfound wealth and freedom to pursue their dreams. My personal hunch is that those few people are already in touch with their purpose!

If exercises like these are ineffective in discovering our deeper purpose, what does work? Through years of iteration and refinement—punctuated by numerous false starts—I have tried dozens of approaches to uncovering purpose in the search for an effective solution. In the end, my associates and I discovered and introduced three questions that have real impact. Each was conceived through trial and error. Each has proven to be a "gateway" to purpose. You will have an opportunity later in the book to apply them for yourself.

1. Magical moments

There are moments in our lives, particularly in childhood and early adulthood, that stand out as intense and special events—moments in which we felt fully alive and engaged with the world. Those moments may have lasted 30 seconds or 30 days. We may have been alone or with friends or family as we experienced them. Those moments may have coincided with major events or very ordinary days. Whatever the case, our whole demeanor changes as we recount those moments and the stories surrounding them. We change from world-weary to intensely alive and engaged. Recounting and accessing those magical moments is one of the best ways to reconnect with our purpose.

2. Challenging experiences

For some, myself included, moments when things are at their worst can point the way to purpose. Challenges on any scale—ranging from personal problems to disasters—can bring us to rock bottom. When we find ourselves in one of these crucible experiences, we rely on our innermost resources for a way out. We reach for and find the purpose that will lead us out of trouble.

3. Activities that excite us over many years

Have you pursued a hobby, sport, or passion for your entire life? Something you never tire of? Whether it's sailing, acting, playing golf, or singing, these activities take us to a powerful place. There's a reason we find them so engrossing and fulfilling. Within these we find a metaphor that captures the core essence of our unique purpose.

These three kinds of experiences have several elements in common. Foremost, as intense experiences they trace well-established neural connections in our brain. When we access them, we don't merely see a two-dimensional movie, we get the entire sensory experience: the smells, tastes, associations, and emotions that were part of it. We re-experience the moments of wonder and insight that are the basic ingredients of purpose. Those moments don't steer us toward something new, they reconnect us to something that is already there and uniquely ours, not a standard Hollywood script of what our purpose "should" be.

Finally, re-experiencing these moments makes us feel deeply alive, engaged, curious, and present. Grown men and women, operating from their stiff and proper adult selves, play with purpose as the curious child inside them takes over. You can see it in their eyes and smiles as the magic within is rekindled. As adults, most of us hide that youngster away. In doing so we closet the thing that energizes and makes us feel alive, that makes others *want* to follow us, that knows which job we should take, or which technology we should bet on. By connecting to our purpose, we put that curious child in the driver's seat.

Each of the next three chapters examines one of the gateways to your personal purpose. One or more of them will help you crack open the door of the room of purpose.

The places where we find our purpose are already within us. Because of that familiarity, many of us tend to undervalue it—most of us value more the things we have not experienced or known. As is often the case, the thing we most search for, we possess already but can't see. We keep searching and not finding it.

I have seen many leaders step into and out of their purpose many times. When they do operate from their purpose, everyone sees it and "gets it" instantly. We know in our gut when someone is operating from purpose—we don't need a checklist to figure it out. They fill the room with their presence. It's not about being loud or expressive; rather, they are operating from this place each person finds where *being* overshadows *doing*. As you read this book and listen to others' stories, you too may step into that place of purpose.

Points to ponder

1. What had been your understanding of purpose before reading this chapter?

2. What do you now "see" that you didn't before about what purpose is and isn't?
3. If you were writing the Declaration of Independence, what would you bring to it that would be your unique gift?
4. If you sailed away from your life today, what would people most miss that couldn't be replaced?

Chapter 3

MAGICAL MOMENTS IN CHILDHOOD

Things that I grew up with stay with me. You start a certain way, and then you spend your whole life trying to find a certain simplicity that you had. It's less about staying in childhood than keeping a certain spirit of seeing things in a different way.

—Tim Burton

Tim Burton is the creative force behind movies ranging from *Beetlejuice* to *Alice in Wonderland*. His words reference one of the greatest access points to purpose, the kid inside us, and remind us that it's not about *being* a kid, but rather how we keep that childlike spirit that allows us to see things in a unique way. If purpose is the unique gift we bring to the world, the curious child inside us probably knows where it is hidden. As obvious as this sounds, none of this was clear ten years ago when I began to look at the role purpose plays in how we lead.

Why are childhood moments so powerful?

According to legend, the Buddha attained enlightenment through remembering a moment in his childhood. As he sat quietly under a tree during a ceremonial plowing festival, the young Siddhartha became interested in watching his breathing. He spontaneously experienced great bliss and became absorbed in a deep meditative state. Years later, after time spent wandering and fruitlessly practicing a range of deprivations, he remembered that beautiful day in his boyhood. Buddha realized that this experience showed him the way to enlightenment.

For most of us, childhood and early adulthood are times of growth and exploration the scope of which will not be repeated. The whole world is new, and we are testing ourselves against it every day. These are the times before the world has defined for us what we "should" be or do. Our education, cultural frame, and view of the world are still developing.

Even a challenging upbringing holds pivotal moments of discovery. They include moments in which we were totally at peace with the world and ourselves, or completely in the flow of being ourselves and doing what we loved and were good at. These are *aha!* moments when the doorway to other possibilities is cracked open. These moments can be incredibly powerful. Recalling them can take us to an entirely different mental and emotional place. What makes some childhood memories such a direct highway to understanding our purpose?

Childhood memories are deeply imprinted

Even if we have not thought of these moments for years, childhood memories can be as fresh and vibrant as something that happened this morning. Intense experiences trace neural connections in our brain. When we revisit them, we enter the moment as if it were in the present. When we evoke strong and powerful childhood memories in ourselves, we re-experience the moments of wonder and insight that are the basic ingredients of purpose. I have watched men and women laugh out loud or cry tears of joy when they connect with the power of these memories.

CHRISTINA—To catalyze people who fly a kite to build the rocket.

Christina Habib is a dynamic leader whose career has been marked by a series of business transformation experiences and turnarounds. She is known for seeing the problems others can't see, taking them by storm, and fixing them for good. Yet after working through one of our sessions, her stated purpose was "To help my team succeed, as I also succeed." As she said it, we all—including Christina—almost yawned at how uncompelling it sounded. Here she was—a big-energy, powerful leader, with peer feedback that was off the charts.

I asked her to tell us a story from her childhood of a beautiful moment that will always be with her. When Christina was very young, her favorite thing was to make kites from bits of paper and fabric and fly them with her father. When the family moved to Bahrain, flying kites was not allowed.

It's Bahrain, 1981, and I am 11 years old. My dad came home one day exhausted, looked at me and asked what was wrong. I told him we can't fly kites anymore; it's boring here. He said, "Come here, let me show you something…" He tore a sheet of paper from my old schoolwork, rolled, twisted, and folded, and turned it into a paper rocket. I was thinking, *Really? Is that all we're gonna do, sit here and pretend my old homework will fly?* He could read my mind. He said, "Kites are a thing of the past. You see, even though they fly high, at some point they get all tangled up in their strings. With a little imagination, you can free them into something that's so much better."

This event took place in 1981, at the time of the first manned space shuttle in the NASA program, but there were no rockets in Bahrain. In that moment, that little girl understood that the kite wasn't important anymore. As Christina revisited this episode, she realized she was in that place where the magic of purpose shows up. Her purpose statement is "To catalyze people who fly a kite to build the rocket."

The minute she said it, she realized why certain roles she had held in her career had been brilliant and others were disasters. She needs to work in an organization where everybody's flying kites, but the kites aren't going to work anymore. If they don't build a rocket, it's over. She is this huge force of energy that comes in and just blows through, and by the time it's over they are building rockets.

As is so often the case, looking at Christina's career through the lens of her purpose brought new perspectives and meaning to episodes in her life that had been confusing. When she went into an organization that already had rockets, she was just one more person. What did she need to be there for? Or if the organization had kites and the kites were working perfectly well, thank you, she equally was the wrong fit. If the organization was struggling to build a rocket and was twisted up in kite strings, she was a masterful gift of transformation. "Steady as you go" wasn't her purpose; for her, leading was about getting business results that no one else even dared suggest. As Christina recounts,

Throughout my professional life, I can see how my purpose has directed me. Every part of a business that I have worked on has never been the same since. My purpose is an inner passion to go from the way things have been to the way they could be. We change the portfolio, the structure, the business and those rockets are still firing. On a personal level, I have been dealing with difficult situations with my marriage and children. When my husband and I grew apart, we decided to stay together and change the shape of our marriage. I talked with both my daughters about their potential and the power of failure: it's okay to fly a rocket that doesn't really work. For me it's not about a record of achievement. It's that ability that they keep hidden due to the fear of failure.

Whenever I fail to live my purpose it results in an incremental change that doesn't last. My purpose is my savings account and those years of challenge are not wasted because I see the benefits of the change.

Retelling these childhood stories allows us to encapsulate our purpose in a way that makes unique sense for us. No one else will say their purpose is "To catalyze people who fly a kite to build the rocket." No one who was not in that room would ever understand it without an explanation. But for Christina, it unlocks meaning and helps her focus her actions.

These magical moments may or may not have been witnessed by others. They may have lasted just a few seconds, yet in those moments we felt the most alive. Remembering them, we almost always smile, as one leader did while recalling a time when she truly believed she had a superpower that could never be mentioned!

There are other great examples of people who arrived at their purpose statement by accessing a childhood memory. If you knew them, you would see how perfectly these stories define the unique purpose of which each is an expression. It's a reminder, too, that while you may think these stories sound trivial to others, they hold great depth of meaning for you. Tapping into them enables these leaders to use the metaphor of the story to see how they lead and when they are operating from their purpose.

Dirk Devos is a senior vice president of marketing who immediately gives the impression of being a person who always leans into what needs to be done. The minute something needs to be figured out, he dives in.

DIRK—Race to the unknown—let's find the whistle!

Dirk had a powerful magical moment in his childhood that perfectly captured the purpose that leads him. He spent 16 years in scouting and loved the annual summer camp, a time spent taking nighttime hikes, building bridges across the river, cooking your own food, going on three-day survival trips, and inventing new games. It was all about the adventure and daring new things—discovering the unknown. For Dirk, the anxiety and excitement around the possibility made it so much fun. His motto was, "How far can we go?" He relished pushing the boundaries and the challenges of difficult situations, using imagination and creativity to come up with solutions or reach the destination. Thrown into tasks that required ingenuity and resourcefulness, he felt he could conquer the world.

There was one game that most captured these elements for him. The final test of the summer required overcoming one's fears and using all the skills of scouting. Late at night, one of the senior guides would go out into the dark woods and blow a whistle. Then, one at a time, without flashlights, the scouts had to stumble through the woods and find the whistle. Adding to the challenge, the person with the whistle would move, so if you just followed the last whistle you would never find it. You had to figure out the pattern and decide where it would be next, not go where you heard it last. Dirk, unlike most of his friends, was excited, not scared. While being in the dark woods alone with no light, surrounded by strange sounds, and chasing after a whistle that kept not being where you hoped it would be was scary for most, Dirk was in heaven. He was not afraid to take on the impossible and was determined to find that guy in the woods. Hour after hour passed and Dirk realized that the key was not to walk toward the whistle but to slow down and just listen. Hearing the other kids get upset when they couldn't find the whistle only reinforced his desire to listen and find the pattern. In the end, he arrived at the place the whistle was, as it was blown in the wee hours of the morning.

> *"Race to the unknown—let's find the whistle!"*—I am typically the one who asks the challenging questions and goes for the whistle with a team without being afraid. Now that I think about it—these are the roles that I felt most comfortable in and was most excited about. It is not about taking risks, because you are focused on where you need to end up—that is, deliver growth by doing things differently.
>
> —*Dirk*

RANJAY—Bring people to center stage, Lights! Camera! Action! We make a difference.

Reconnecting to purpose by way of a childhood magical moment ends up being a significant "unlock." When I met Ranjay, he was a very serious guy. A senior vice president of human resources for a global corporation, he faced enormous responsibilities and challenges in his role. People saw him as a strongly values-driven leader who for the most part didn't smile, at least not until he reconnected to his purpose. Yes, we can hide from our purpose, but it is always there waiting for us to access it.

When Ranjay talked about his magical childhood moments, I was struck by how transformed he was. Also, he didn't just have one moment, he had a whole series of moments from his childhood. It turns out that, growing up, Ranjay *loved* the stage. His earliest memory is of being on stage, being in the spotlight, either solo or as part of the cast of a play. His childhood was completely consumed by performing. When he didn't have a script he liked, he would write one himself and then present it. He performed as a stand-up comedian and ran for president of his high school student union. These activities brought him much more joy than academics ever would, even though he was an outstanding student. It was a profound experience to watch Ranjay tell these stories; we watched him transform from a deeply serious man to the most energized and curious boy. It was as if someone had turned on the lights in Ranjay. He had completely forgotten this part of his life and how it had shaped who he was. I watched years of heaviness lift from his shoulders as he reconnected with his purpose. This insight into what gives Ranjay his "ultimate kick" gave him a compass that he didn't have before. Ranjay's purpose statement is *"Bring people to center stage, Lights! Camera! Action! We make a difference."*

The impact of this has been profound for Ranjay. He now takes significant risks, placing bets on key people and bringing them to center stage. He loves to promote people two or three levels, causing others to scratch their heads and wonder what happened. Coaching and supporting these individuals have now become key expressions of his purpose. He realized that he was where he was in his career because people placed a big bet on him. The first time he felt this was when people around him supported him to be center stage when he was a kid. Now he reminds himself, "Let's bring people to center stage and let's make a big bet and invest in them." He realized that that if a candidate can start running from day one, you aren't really building that person—they are already ready, they don't need your help, and they will want to leave in three years. If you take a big bet, that person will stay for a long time and leave behind a legacy, as Ranjay has done. That doesn't mean it's not painful for the first two years. Ranjay realized that those tough first years are key parts of bringing people to center stage.

I believe we all deserve some time in our career to work for a Ranjay. I know that the times I have had someone like Ranjay in my life have been my most empowering and satisfying job experiences. If he hadn't reconnected to his childhood magical moments and his purpose, many others would most likely not be at center stage today.

Our purpose will always bring us home

We return to Christina, our rocket-powered purposeful leader, to bring this chapter to a close. After reconnecting with her purpose, Christina has seen its power in her current role.

> You ask me why my purpose now? It's in times like this, in a mad VUCA world and a struggling business, where people are tied up in their kite strings holding on to what used to work. Only a rocket can dare show people the possibility in themselves to land on the moon. The world as we knew it isn't there anymore.
>
> We live our lives searching for meaning to exist and do what we do. It's hard to find, and easy to lose, in this demanding autopilot life.

Christina's story does not end with the moment she reconnected with her purpose and found her purpose statement.

You may remember the man who pulled me out of despair over a kite with the possibility of making a rocket in the middle of a nation that couldn't imagine them. One December 4, I spontaneously Googled for some rocket PowerPoint slides. I had no idea why I had a sudden compulsion to waste this time in the middle of a heavy business and life crisis that week. Today I remembered: December 4 was the day that man—my father—passed away. I never managed to say a proper goodbye or how much I loved him, and I had tortured myself for it for eight years. Now I've come to peace with the fact that we don't need goodbyes. Somehow, he lives on, in me and in that silly PowerPoint slide. "Christina, don't worry about the kite. Let's make a rocket."

Points to ponder

1. When you were a kid, what activity or moment brought you the most joy and satisfaction? (This could be one specific moment, a specific activity, or a list of experiences.)
2. Describe one of those moments in vivid detail. Write about it as if you were back in the experience right now.
3. What are the key elements to the story that stand out?
4. What emotions are evoked as you remember this moment?

Chapter 4

CRUCIBLE STORIES

That which does not kill us makes us stronger.

—Friedrich Nietzsche

For some of us, our purpose shines most brightly in our darkest moments. Our lives are summed up in the age-old proverb "A smooth sea never made a skilled sailor." In *Geeks and Geezers*, authors Warren Bennis and Robert Thomas describe crucibles as intense experiences that test us to our very limits. "The skills required to conquer adversity and emerge stronger and more committed than ever are the same ones that make for extraordinary leaders." Our crucible experiences can be the very experiences that force us to finally "show up" and step into our purpose.

My own ability to discover and operate from my purpose is deeply rooted in some of the most challenging moments in my life. Remembering magical moments from my childhood has not led me to understand my purpose. My passions over time are connected to my purpose, but only from the perspective of knowing what my crucible moments have shown me. It isn't possible to be a truly self-aware leader if you haven't examined the times you have been most tested and what those events show you about who you are. If your purpose isn't to be found in those moments, then it's probably not your purpose, is it?

The power of the crucible

It wasn't until I encountered a couple of remarkable women that I saw the role crucibles can take in defining our purpose. So, before I tell you my own story, I want to introduce you to Jacqui and Stacey. Early in my journey to understand where purpose comes from, they taught me the power of our crucible stories as a special place to find purpose, that unique gift that we bring to the world.

JACQUI—Through tenacity, deliver brilliance.

As the new general manager in New Zealand for a big box retailer similar to Home Depot, Jacqui, a woman in a very male world, needed to lead an important business turnaround. I was genuinely curious to uncover the purpose that was driving her to lead confidently in what others thought was an unwinnable assignment. I wasn't disappointed.

When Jacqui shared her crucible stories, I knew we were in the place of purpose. These stories had none of the hushed tone of a tough story we have not visited for a long time that, once told, we are relieved and simply thankful that we learned a hard lesson in a challenging situation. On the contrary, Jacqui was ecstatic as she told these stories. As I listened, I realized for the first time that I wasn't the only one whose purpose came from these sacred stories of death and rebirth.

When she was just 15, Jacqui discovered she was pregnant; her boyfriend was a 29-year-old rookie professional soccer player. Good Catholics, the couple married, and not for love. Over the next nine years she watched her life fall apart as her husband's soccer career was sidelined by injuries and he turned to the bottle. With the bottle came physical violence. At the age of 25, eight months pregnant with her third child, she took her two girls and left. She remembers standing in front of a pharmacy in the light rain—pregnant, with two girls and little more than the clothes on their backs. For the next three and half months they lived in a shelter. Then, with the addition of a newborn boy, she received housing assistance from the shelter. Standing over a pile of boxes full of items mostly donated by strangers, she watched her kids as they slept that first night in their new home. In that instant, Jacqui had a "wow" moment, a moment of clarity that she has never experienced since. Jacqui realized that she was most at peace when she was dealing with situations that most other people just couldn't even imagine dealing with.

That last sentence probably wasn't what you were expecting after reading her story, and it sure wasn't what I expected to hear, either. Every day, she needed to figure out how to feed herself and her kids and put together a life that was completely unlike the one she had been living. She got back on her feet, pursued a career, and raised her kids. Surprisingly, she had never shared this story until we sat together; in the telling, purpose appeared. She knew it and I knew it, and Jacqui's purpose will be clear to you soon, too.

We often have more than one crucible experience

Her next story comes from the economic recession of 2008. By then Jacqui had become a very successful senior executive for a global retailer that had recently opened its anchor store in Hong Kong. Unfortunately, the store needed to be closed, and fast. Jacqui decided to take on the role of closing the store, with the personal goal of finding all 30 employees new jobs. In normal times, this would take three to six months. But during the 2008 recession, when no one knew where the bottom would be, nobody was hiring. This was a culture in which no one got laid off, and the language barrier was almost as significant as the cultural ones. When she announced to the team what was happening, it was clear that few understood what she was saying. The global organization didn't care—"Just let them go" was their stance. Jacqui decided that wasn't who she is. She personally walked with 12 members of the team to key interviews in hopes of their getting the few jobs that were out there. Nobody was asking her to do this, but to Jacqui these people were no different from her own kids. She would do whatever it took to make it right for each of these employees. To be clear, these were not people she had worked with for years. It had been months. But Jacqui only knows one speed. One of the happiest days in her life was the day she closed the store for the last time, with everyone placed in a new position.

Here's the final story about Jacqui. You must be wondering what her purpose is…by now it should be getting clear. What might it be?

Jacqui's next job was with another global retailer. Her desire was to become an area manager but even though she delivered results making it clear she was one of the best performers, others were promoted to key roles. Finally, the managing director asked her to meet, looked her in the eye, and said, "We want you to be an area manager. We need a woman and you are the best that we have." Jacqui had worked very hard to get where she was and had no interest in being the token women on a senior team. She resigned the next day, after six years of giving her best.

Some of us are wired differently. What would be a disaster for some is experienced as a triumph by others. Part of Jacqui's unique gift is how she operates in challenging moments. The common thread we uncovered as we discussed her stories became her purpose statement: "Through tenacity, deliver brilliance." If all hell is breaking loose, I want to be standing next to Jacqui.

Crucibles weave a pattern in our lives

The pattern across several crucible experiences is what can help us see the purpose that has been leading us in these challenging times. None of us chooses where we are born or the world we face as we grow up. What we can choose is how we relate to it and how we bring our purpose to our journey.

STACEY—To ignite the worthy fight and blow your hair back.

At the age of seven, Stacey was living her crucible. Having moved from New York to Texas, she was a fish out of water with a Yankee accent. Her family boomeranged back to the Northeast after about a year, when she again found herself in a new school try-ing to make new friends. Her parents were consumed over many years by taking care of a sick family member, doing what needed to be done and often gone, so Stacey paved her own way. She was the one her parents didn't need to worry about. She found a level of tenacity and resilience that drove her to get straight As and play varsity sports as well as edit the school newspaper.

Twenty years later, Stacey was working in marketing com-munications when she decided she needed a new challenge. She set her sights on joining the Corporate Audit staff—something that no one from her background had successfully done before. Her first hurdle was to convince the senior leaders to give her a shot—and they did, over a four-week "pilot" assignment. She achieved passing marks in her pilot, and on to the Corporate Audit staff she went, accepting a finance job. Little did she know, this was like joining the Special Forces. It was a steep learning curve, and for a couple of years she managed on only two or three hours of sleep a night; she was never in one place for long, operating on a basis of 100 percent global travel. She felt as if she were the dumbest person in the room much of the time as she just tried to survive and learn. For years she wanted to quit every day, but she kept going.

Next, she came face-to-face with death during the birth of her first son. As she was having eclampsia seizures on the oper-ating table and the doctors were strapping her down, she stared into the overhead lights and thought, "Wow, is this how it ends?" When she woke up, doctors with ghost-white faces told her that she had been very close to full kidney and liver shutdown. This forced her to slow down and take care of herself (and her baby) for the first time in her life. Work had to come second, which was not easy for Stacey.

The last story she shared was that in her twenties she was diagnosed as a carrier of the BRCA1 mutation connected to breast and ovarian cancer. After her mom was diagnosed with advanced ovarian cancer at a relatively young age, Stacey learned that she had an 87 percent lifetime risk of breast cancer and a 54 percent chance of ovarian cancer. She was the youngest patient at Yale hospital to ever have a prophylactic mastectomy, and later opted for a risk-reducing prophylactic hysterectomy in her thirties. She turned this horrible reality into a gift that she could give away—she chose to support other young women in the same situation by taking a seat on Bright Pink's nonprofit board and becoming an education ambassador.

Stacey tells her crucible stories from a place of enormous energy and spark. After looking at these stories and the energy and curiosity that she always brings to these moments in her life, she articulated a very appropriate purpose statement: *"To ignite the worthy fight and blow your hair back."* This intense purpose is the perfect antidote to all of Stacey's challenges. If you meet her, you will immediately know what I mean. There is more intense energy radiating from her than from just about anyone I have ever met. If you have hair, it will be blown back when you are around her!

Both Stacey and Jacqui go looking for the adventures that others run away from. Their purpose has them most energized when they face situations that other people would see as disasters. In a way, that is the beautiful gift of purpose. Each of us has a unique response to events. Because it is different from others, it allows us to see possibilities that others can't.

Seeing my own youth as a crucible

Now for my own crucible journey. I started first grade in a small elementary school outside Chattanooga, Tennessee, in the late 1960s. I was far from any of the events we associate with that period in time. My world was the world of a first-grade teacher who knew how to use a wooden paddle. For reasons I will never know, she decided that I, more than anyone else in that classroom, needed a weekly dose of it. Sometimes I did something that warranted being reminded of the rules, but most of the time I hadn't done anything. She would say she was just making up for the times she didn't catch me. You can imagine what that does to a six-year-old. I remember realizing that nothing I did or didn't do was going to change the situation. The idea of telling my parents didn't even enter my head. What I decided to do was to dig deep and be smarter than anyone else.

I needed to go to a place inside myself that she couldn't enter; luckily, I really was at home inside myself. If there's no home outside, find it within. The point isn't whether it was fair or just, but how I responded to an inescapable situation. Reading became my escape starting in the first grade, increasing in importance every year.

Life became much better after that and I would say I had a relatively "normal" set of adventures until I was 15 years old, when I was again in a tough place. In 1975, in the middle of my ninth-grade year, we moved to Charleston, South Carolina, and I was dropped into one of the worst school systems in the nation. We were living in a basement apartment after having lived in a nice house. My parents were at a low point in their relationship and their jobs. I was a nerdy, lonely kid and as lost a soul as you could find.

One day I rode my bike to a bookstore and somehow found myself in the section that housed philosophy and whatever "self-help" was called before it took over half the bookstore shelves. I started reading the great philosophers, from Aristotle to Heidegger, diving into stories about everything from levitating Buddhist monks to Mahatma Gandhi. As I read, I was struck by the overall theme: Our potential as a human being is ten times what most of us achieve and experience. These stories were about people who had done things that seemed impossible, but they had done them anyway. I felt as far away from these people as any 15-year-old could, but at the same time I finally felt "home." I remember thinking that I was no longer alone. Many of the stories included being lost, rejected, or unwanted, which I could totally relate to. Yet they were stories of redemption and renewal.

I realized that I could spend my life as a victim, or I could focus my life on discovering what we are capable of being. I remember having that thought and making the choice. Did I think, "Wow, now I know my purpose!"? No, all I was focused on was finding some light in what felt like a very dark life, no more and no less. It's only in looking back that we see where purpose shows up for us.

Externally, my life didn't change a great deal, but my relationship to the world did. I realized that the events that happened were just that: events. It's the meaning we make out of them that determines how we react and what we do. I began reading everything I could on the topic, and when real-world examples didn't help, *Dune* or *The Lord of the Rings* did. Actually, *The Lord of the*

Rings carried me through many tough times as a clumsy adolescent. It was less an escape and more a reminder that we can all step into our bigger selves no matter how bad things seem in the moment.

In 1977, I decided to learn to meditate. I looked "meditation" up in the Yellow Pages, that 1970s paper equivalent of a Google search. If monks could meditate and slow down their heart rates and levitate, I wanted to do so, too. My purpose was working on me; I just didn't have any idea what it was.

My next crucible was my first job out of college. I graduated with a computer science degree and moved to Boston to work for Digital Equipment Corporation (now HP), probably the most unstructured workplace of its time. For six months, nobody told me what to do or much of anything. I had achieved straight As in college and had an incredible mentor in one professor, Dr. Hayden Porter. He looked like Gandalf in *The Lord of the Rings* and many times I really felt like the character Frodo. Dr. Porter pushed me and pushed me and never stopped, which you could say was a very positive crucible experience.

That first job, I was Frodo with no Gandalf to be found. I was so miserable that I felt like I was in prison when I went to work. So, I did what I always do: I went and searched for wisdom. This time, being in Boston, instead of reading books I could hear this wisdom directly. The teachers covering the gamut—from the most transformed person on the planet, the Dalai Lama, to MIT Sloan school professor Edgar Schein, whose insights on organization culture change I still use today.

Back at work as this all percolated in me, I decided to take a course from some of the famous people who created the best

NGUYEN, THUY HONG DANG

NGUYEN, THUY HONG DANG

Hold Slip

Fraserview Branch Library
06/08/21 03:30PM

NGUYEN, THUY HONG DANG

Item: 31383115394440
Call No.: 658.4092 C8BL
Leading from purpose /

Hold for 8 days.

computer hardware and software of that time, the VAX-11/780, a machine that had as large an impact on the computer industry as Apple Macintosh did a few years later. The creator of the VAX operating system (David Cutler, who went on to create the Windows NT operating system) said he landed the job to create the precursor to the VAX operating system (RSX) by showing up at the first meeting with 50,000 lines of code already written. Hearing him tell that story, I had a significant *aha!* moment. My biggest insights always come when the crucible is at its worst, and this is the message I heard: *You can create your destiny versus being served with it.* I felt in some way more "home" at that moment than I had in a couple of years.

What has emerged from the fire?

I didn't discover my purpose statement until I was in my mid-forties and I was working on *The Discover Your True North Fieldbook* with Bill George. Taking responsibility for the chapter on purpose had a way of focusing the mind. Purpose is a ruthless taskmaster. The wording of my purpose statement is *"To wake you up, and have you finally be home."* Why those words as opposed to all the other words out there? I am most alive when I am waking someone up to his or her deeper self, just as others did for me in my darkest moments—whether it was Gandalf in *The Lord of the Rings* or the creator of the VAX operating system. I always found that waking up to a deeper truth was like being really home. Here I am, years later, looking at those experiences and beginning to see how my purpose showed up for me in the work I was doing.

I meet people all the time who are in the middle of a crucible experience. When I do, I smile because I know that a deeper truth is waiting for them around the corner: their purpose. When it is revealed, most people are amazed; they finally feel okay with who they are at their core. They are finally "home."

For leaders, there is probably nothing more important than the certainty that, instead of chasing after someone else's Holy Grail, what you seek is there within you. I love the end of *The Wizard of Oz*. Dorothy is ready to return home—after a heck of a crucible experience—but doesn't know how to. The good witch Glinda descends from the sky and says, "Just tap your red slippers together—you always had the power to go home." In some ways, that is my purpose. To help you realize you always have the power to be at home with who you really are. Teaching programs on authentic leadership and purpose is a strategy through which I live my purpose.

Steel is tempered through fire. Coming through difficult moments or long rocky periods in your life can forge a purpose like no other. Examining my crucible stories answered so many questions about who I was, why I had done many of the things I had, and where I am going, as it has for many others.

Your purpose is always leading you. The opportunity is to fully own it. Some of us find that our purpose is most engaged and available when what others see as a crucible experience is, for us, an opportunity to lead from our purpose. I hope those of you who, like me, need a little kick in the pants to find heaven, will explore your crucible stories to shine a light onto your own purpose and, in the process, feel more at "home" with who you are.

Points to ponder

1. Describe two or three of your most challenging life experiences. These can be either personal or professional moments when you were tested the most.
2. What would be missing from your life without these experiences?
3. What are the gifts that these experiences bring to your life?
4. What within you was key to getting through these experiences?

Chapter 5

FINDING PURPOSE THROUGH PASSION

> Our passions, simply stated, are our curiosities—those
> things we care most deeply about. Whatever form they
> take, passions are identified by their vitality. They are
> "alive" and we feel them deeply. A passion moves us to
> action in the world. Moreover, a passion doesn't quit but
> keeps recurring in our thinking and experiences.
>
> —Richard J. Leider

Our final access point to purpose is one that for many is the
key to uncovering that which has been leading us all our lives.
Richard Leider, a colleague who has written extensively about
the connection between passion and purpose, explains that the
actions that continually bring us the most vitality in our life
often reveal a compelling access point to our purpose.

We all have passions, and many of them change over time.
For a passion to help us connect to the purpose that leads us,
it needs to have been with us for some time. It may not be an
activity we pursue today, but it has been an essential part of us at
some foundational point in our life. Whether it is football, running, singing, skiing, or playing the violin, the key is the level of
vitality and energy we get or got from doing it.

We approach these activities differently. For instance, we don't see the instruction manuals for our passions as necessary evils keeping us from doing what we really want to do. We relate to these manuals and guidebooks in a very different way. The lessons and stories of others who have gone before us are what we read on vacation. They make us feel vital and reconnected to something important to us.

For most of us, these activities have little or nothing to do with what we do for a living, what type of role we have, or even what we are good at. It's something we love doing for the sake of doing it. In this passion is a set of metaphors and ways of seeing the world that capture our gift, that purpose that leads us. Just like the other access points of magical moments in our child-hood or our crucible experiences, our passions are something we have done so frequently that the neural connections associated with them are deeply installed. The visual images, emotions, and muscle memory are vivid, and unique. What about all those other people in the world who have the same passion we do? Even with the same passion, we each have a unique way we experience it and relate to the world. No two football players are the same; no two soloists interpret a concerto the same way.

Reconciling the road not taken

JOHN—To always be the lead violinist in the orchestra.

John felt torn about his life choices. At the pinnacle of his corporate career as the SVP of marketing, with an ad budget in the tens of millions of dollars, John is "the man," yet he felt conflicted.

When he was 21, he was on track to become a world-class violinist. He fell in love, married, had kids, and put his dream on hold. He received a master's in marketing and quickly moved up the ranks, much faster than his peers, to one of the top marketing jobs. Now John is 45, and that voice in his head keeps asking if he took the wrong path. Like the narrator in Robert Frost's poem "The Road Not Taken," John saw

> *Two roads diverged in a yellow wood,*
> *And sorry I could not travel both . . .*

He thinks, "What would it be like if I had stayed with the violin? Would I now play first violin for a major orchestra?" Evenings and weekends, John plays the violin and wonders.

When John talked about playing the violin, his whole being lit up. It was electric. We were in the room of purpose—the challenge was to understand how he could access that place always. The words help us access our purpose, and the words must mean something very powerful to help us connect with purpose.

Somewhere in John's experience of playing the violin was the key to the room of purpose that we were looking for. For many of us—whether it's playing an instrument, singing, skiing, or playing golf—there is something we do that transcends space and time. That is the place where purpose resides.

I asked John to describe why he imagined he would make a world-class first violinist. The characteristics he listed were the same ones that had helped him rocket to the top of his profession. He described someone who was exactly on time, could bring the whole orchestra together, create magical moments, and be in service to the conductor. Explaining this, he showed the same energy I had seen when he described playing the violin. Not surprisingly, his description exactly matched what others had said about him in his most recent peer/boss performance review. This was how others saw John, too.

John's purpose is "*To always be the lead violinist in the orchestra.*" When we looked at how he led and lived his life, he has always operated as the first violin. Some of the time, he actually played the violin. The minute he had that insight, John realized that the greatest paradox of his life was no more. He didn't have to wonder if he should have followed a different path. There was only one path—his purpose—that had been leading him all this time and that he expressed in every facet of his life. The thing he was dreaming of becoming had been who he was and always would be. When John told his boss his purpose statement ("To always be the lead violinist in the orchestra"), his boss laughed out loud, then told him that was exactly why they gave him the big job.

Each of us is a paradox, a combination of seemingly contradictory elements. We sometimes have a hard time accepting some parts of ourselves, or finding a place to let those parts "breathe." One of the greatest gifts of purpose is that it resolves the paradox of who we are and allows us to go from hiding a part of ourselves to feeling fully integrated. That integration and congruency are what we most want to see in any leader.

This is the power of purpose. It's more about the unique way that we do what we do than it is about the actual job. John is now able to play the violin and experience it as a full expression of his purpose, as is taking a key role in a big meeting to prepare an ad for the Super Bowl. Our purpose works through us, no matter what we are doing. The gift of knowing it is to be at peace with what we are and the magic that we bring to the world around us.

Harnessing the power of a passion

So, what is the thing you have had passion for over an extended period? For some of us, our passion has been a sport we play that has been an integral part of our identity. The many hours of practice and playing and the lessons learned provide a rich field for us to identify the purpose that leads us—especially when life isn't always focused on making us happy. We have a deep network of neural connections and pathways that put us fully in the game of purpose when we step back onto that field.

PETER—Play champion league everywhere, every day.

This was the case for Peter, the oldest of three boys, whose parents should never have married. Things at home were always tense, and playing soccer was his refuge. When he was in college his parents finally divorced—a very messy divorce involving lots of fighting and an ugly court case. While still going to school, he stepped in to mediate the divorce between his parents. Living at home with his mom and dealing with a divorce wasn't the normal life of a college kid. With that, soccer became even more important. Amid all the challenges at home he was playing first-class soccer in a very competitive environment.

At this point you could say that his story probably isn't so different from others. Many people play soccer, football, baseball, or some other sport—but is that really an access point to their purpose?

Peter's lifelong passion for the game went deeper than most. He was on the same town club from the time he was 7 until the age of 34, sometimes traveling 75 miles three times a week to practice and go to games. No one was paid, and, unlike other teams, there were no ex-professional soccer players to depend on. Yet Peter's team won the championship of their amateur league in Holland—twice. Time after time, he turned down promotions so he could stay in Holland and remain on the team, taking less attractive general management roles over potential fast-track expertise paths. His purpose statement is *"Play champion league everywhere, every day."*

For Peter, "champion league" refers to playing at the highest performance level while nurturing a strong relationship with each player. Today, over 200 managers work for him, and he makes it his goal to connect with every one of them in a personal way. Being close to people is his leadership style on *and* off the field. He'll stand above when necessary, but he really likes to be just part of the team as a senior player, to stay close and see the big picture.

To be clear, Peter's purpose isn't really to play champion league soccer. That's a metaphor, a phrase that reminds him of a way of operating that is who he always has been. Purpose shows up in the things we have a deep passion for because they are expressions of that purpose. Things that have energized us, or that we are passionate about, have built complex sets of experiences, wisdom, and mindset that powerfully represent the purpose that leads through us.

At one point, Peter left Holland and became the number-two leader for the Thailand office. His management team wasn't great, but after interviewing many external candidates, he realized what he had was the best there was. So, he decided to fully step into his purpose and lead from that place. Just as he had done in Holland with a soccer team nobody expected to perform but that in the end delivered, that team turned around the business.

CLAUDIO—To fly on water.

Our final example brings us back to the power of purpose and the paradox that each of us encompasses. Claudio's purpose statement is *"To fly on water."* I know those words don't make any sense. His purpose is a paradox, but it didn't start that way. It took a while to get to it because he was stuck on his purpose being "To create value for the company and business, while building happiness in people's lives." Remember, your purpose must work for you in all parts of your life. We lead in everything we do, not just where we get paid. Sure, happiness is a good thing and clearly it was a key element of his purpose. Yet, as with many executives, he was stuck in the business mindset. He was a very serious man and happiness didn't seem to be his special gift. In asking him who he was at home, I learned that Claudio has a special-needs son in his twenties who lives with him and his wife.

So, who was he both at home and at work that expressed his purpose? Clearly, his son could have been a crucible experience, yet Claudio didn't see it that way. His magical moments in his childhood didn't jump out or bring much to the table. It turns out that Claudio loves swimming. Growing up, it was the one thing he loved to do. When things with his son became challenging as they discovered his diagnosis, swimming was his place of tranquility.

Claudio doesn't like to just swim; instead, what he loves most is something that he experiences only rarely, the feeling of flying on water when he swims. In that moment, the water disappears, and he can swim lap after lap without stopping. The rest of the time is the daily discipline and commitment of swimming in the water. Without the experience of flying on water, all the effort would not be as meaningful and fulfilling for him. When the group—his colleagues who know him well—heard this, they said, "There you are; that truly is what you bring to meetings that no one else brings. You make the impossible possible and make it look effortless." His response was, "Yes, that is how it looks and sometimes feels, but it is the daily practice done over years that makes it possible." You could see his level of discipline, commitment, and mastery combined in his purpose of "To fly on water."

Considering this, his whole career made sense. In one specific example, he had to close manufacturing plants in France. Of all the places in the world that you might have to close a plant and lay people off, France is one of the most difficult. The legal system makes it extremely difficult to let people go. The company had too many plants in France and Claudio was chosen to lead the transition. He decided to share the plan with the trade unions long before he legally had to. Telling them that to strengthen the business some of the plants had to be closed was a tough moment. The feedback was direct and very intense. Claudio was now the least popular guy in the company. Establishing the new structure took more than a year and required discipline and patience every day. At one point, there were riots that stranded the management team in the main office overnight. Slowly, Claudio was able to convince the trade unions to agree to the plans and even help execute them. The result was a number of years of growth in the business that was far ahead of the market. When he left, the trade union leader delivered a speech saying Claudio had gone from being the worst thing that had ever happened to them to the best! All through this time, swimming was Claudio's teacher and "to fly on water" was his core essence.

A long-held and deep passion is the third access point through which many connect to the purpose that has always been there waiting to be owned. For some of us, these experiences are metaphors for the unique gift that we bring to the world. Whether we access our purpose through passions, childhood memories, or remembering our crucibles, the challenge is to live and lead from it.

Points to ponder

We all have passions in our life, pursuits that bring out the curious child inside each of us. As you look at your journey in life, think of those things that have stayed with you over time. Just as our purpose never runs away, these passions are with us throughout our lives. These activities may have no redeeming quality other than you really love doing them. Your passion isn't necessarily what you are best at or paid to do.

1. What is your passion? (cooking, playing the violin, singing, dancing, painting, sailing, etc.)
2. Describe a particular moment when you were fully experiencing your passion.
3. Describe two other moments when you were fully experiencing your passion.
4. How do you feel in these moments?
5. Who are you in these moments?

PART II

FINDING YOUR PURPOSE

➡ SO, WHAT IS YOUR PURPOSE?

The Way It Is
There's a thread you follow. It goes among
things that change. But it doesn't change.
People wonder about what you are pursuing.
You have to explain about the thread.
But it is hard for others to see.
While you hold it you can't get lost.
Tragedies happen; people get hurt
or die; and you suffer and get old.
Nothing you do can stop time's unfolding.
You don't ever let go of the thread.

—William Stafford, "The Way It Is," 1993

Instead of suggesting that you wait until the end of the book, I want to help you here, now, in the middle of the journey, to begin to access your purpose. The second half of the book is about the impact purpose has made on many leaders and their lives; having an idea of what your own purpose is will make reading their stories even more meaningful.

The lines by William Stafford capture what the true gift of purpose is. It is the one thing that doesn't change; it is waiting to lead us through all of life's adventures. You are the one who must find it, and when you have it, you can't get lost. In the last few compelling lines, Stafford reminds us that as everything else gets stripped away, we must not let go of the thread. It's the one thing that is the core essence of who we are.

Let's go find your thread!

What does an engaging purpose statement look like?

Faced with the task of crafting "the perfect" purpose statement, most people freeze up. Many of us fall back into the comfortable land of mission statements and high-flown phraseology. To help you step out of the normal wordsmithing mindset that we all tend to get into, let's start with an out-of-the-box example and work from there.

$$\text{RIKKYA—Input} = \int \text{Data} * \text{People @me.}$$

I am rarely surprised by anyone's purpose statement, but this was the first time I had seen purpose presented as a mathematical equation. Yet why should we limit ourselves to just using words? It makes complete sense, as Rikkya (who works for a bank in Amsterdam) is a fabulously nerdy mathematician.

Why is this Rikkya's purpose?

I'm the integrator of data and people to achieve impact. At work, this means that my team and I analyze data to identify opportunities for cost savings. We then work with the business to make these happen, to improve the cost-income ratio of the company.

In my personal life, this means anything from starting the nerdy book club to watching documentaries with my partner. I love data, working with people, and seeing something come out of that combination. Nerd power.

When Rikkya created her purpose statement, you could see and feel that, all at once, everything came together and made sense for her. She had the confidence to author an equation. She is using her passion for math as the access key to her purpose.

I sometimes think that each person's purpose is similar to Cinderella's glass slipper. It's not a standard size 6. It fits one person and one person only. Yet many of us try, like Cinderella's stepsisters, to cram our foot into someone else's slipper or take one "off the shelf." I believe we all have a natural "sniff test" as to when something is authentic. Yet, over the years I have been amazed by how we all first grab on to a set of tired and inauthentic phrases. Here are some bad examples:

- To help my team succeed, as I also succeed
- Synergize you to be your greatest potential
- Making things world class as we all succeed
- Empowering you as I empower myself and we leverage our diversity
- Continually and consistently develop and facilitate the growth and development of myself and others, leading to great performance

These have all the right words, and lots of them. I must confess that, early on, I helped create these lifeless purpose statements. It is so easy to just come up with a purpose statement that has all the right HR words yet actually means nothing. The words themselves aren't the problem, but when you ask people to explain why they picked those words, it falls apart. When they stand in front of the group and say the words, the effect is totally flat. Ho-hum. You could pick a random set from a list of leadership buzzwords and get something just as tired. It took me a number of years to figure out how to help leaders create a purpose statement that, when they expressed it, helped them access the unique room of purpose that is theirs alone.

I remember Allen, a senior leader who initially suggested this for his purpose statement:

Making things world class as we all succeed.

This is how Allen explained his purpose: "One must always be world class, or what's the point? And the reason I lead is to succeed." Listening to him was like sitting in a typical leadership training course and hearing those words being played back to me. Okay, so *lead/succeed* sort of rhymes, but there was no authenticity. Worse, he said it as if it was a question, asking me if it sounded good enough. The next day we got to solid ground and ended up with Allen's updated purpose statement:

ALLEN—The pathfinder, taking us to places where no path has been found and getting us back in one piece.

Why is this Allen's purpose?

All my life I have found myself in places where everyone feels lost, including me, whether on a trip or running a technology project. There comes a point when there is no path and I get the rest of us to take the next step. Each step we learn something we didn't know before, and before long we realize there is a path.

Just the day before, Allen and I probably went through twenty iterations before we landed on the pathfinder metaphor. When we landed on it we realized we had been right in the middle of his purpose, without a path, as we tried to access his purpose! When he told his team they all laughed—"Yep, that is so you."

The gift that you really are needs to peek out from the words. If we define our purpose with the latest popular jargon, then my greatest fear will come true: purpose will go the way of many other leadership fads; everyone will "have one" and it will end up in the junk pile with all the other discarded toys.

Here are a couple more examples:

MAX—I am a [LEGO]-poet who, with words, builds a [BRIDGE] from [HEAD/BRAIN] to [HEART].

Why is this Max's purpose?

As a kid, I loved to play with Legos—build, break down, rebuild—until I thought the construction was finished. Sometimes it became something concrete, sometimes it spoke to one's imagination.

Playing with Legos has gradually shifted into a passion for writing—playing with words; write, delete, rewrite—until I think the poem is finished. Sometimes it contains a clear message, sometimes it speaks to the imagination.

During the process of shaping my purpose I discovered that I approach my passion for writing in the same way as my work: trying to deliver quality, using my imagination (therefore using pictures), finding ways to appoint and combine thoughts and making connections people didn't think of themselves. I experience that, by doing so, I connect myself with them and can make a difference: like a Lego poet who, with words, builds a bridge from head to heart.

Yes, it's okay to use more than words in your purpose statement. Notice how much power a picture has. As a side note, I am always amazed by how many people have childhood magical experiences playing with Legos that end up being part of their purpose statements.

For some of us, the movies provide an access point to our purpose. Jedi knights, starship captains, dragon slayers, and then some: these metaphors pop out from our childhood magical moments or passion stories. For example, Michal runs a country organization for a major *Fortune* 500 organization and found his purpose in a baseball movie.

MICHAL—Play Moneyball.

Why is this Michal's purpose?

Unlock the potential of underdog teams, organizations, brands. Play with the (perceived) weaker team or the one having low chances to succeed, and by analytics, collecting insights, building strategy and making it happen. At the same time being pragmatic, flexible in tactics not in direction. Mastering the logic, concept, direction but asking for help in execution, activities. Not (always) being with the team and sharing emotions but always planning and supporting behind the scenes. Engaging as much as possible great people, assets, market but undervalued or unexplored by others. Enjoying (playing) the process to get to the goal, but being reserved and planning next steps already before, once seeing the goal will be achieved. Communicating as much as needed to engage and achieve objective, but not enjoying being in the spotlight.

When I was working with Michal, the thread that appeared over and over again was of being the underdog. Growing up, he would purposefully switch teams to be on the one that everyone thought was the worst and relish in their overturning the status quo. *Moneyball: The Art of Winning an Unfair Game* by Michael Lewis, and the film based on it, both wonderfully describe a way of seeing the world that Michal feels captures his gift. Is Michal exactly like Lewis's description of Oakland A's manager Billy Beane? No, but that's not the point. The words are an access key, not the room of purpose itself. Every time Michal says his purpose statement, he gets the biggest grin and then he gets back to leading from his purpose.

Some of us store our purpose statement away in a box for safekeeping. Geert is the head of treasury for a large multinational bank and has a unique purpose statement:

GEERT—To keep digging for the medals.

Why is this Geert's purpose?

History, corporate history, and corporate memory are close to my heart. It doesn't matter if you make mistakes, but let's learn from them and not make them again. Finding World War I medals as a young boy started to trigger in me a passion for this history and what we can learn from it. It was a start of a lifelong training journey, learning myself and coaching many others.

When Geert told his wife his purpose, she asked him the question we all wanted to ask: Did he still have the medal? When he got home he showed her the medal that he had saved in a box for safekeeping. Nowadays, the kid who found the medal is the same one who finds the funding needed to finance the running of a very successful bank.

To be clear, the purpose that is leading you doesn't need to be provocative or "out there" to be effective. One of the most purposeful leaders I know is David Hopley, who spent most of his life as a soldier and ended his military career as second in command of UK Special Forces.

DAVID—To be the beacon on the rock that emboldens you to be who you truly are.

Why is this David's purpose?

Beacon—I've been in a lot of "dark places," professionally and personally (e.g., losing men under my command; sudden death of my first wife; a son who almost died and another who struggled with his sexuality). Somehow, I always found a way back and helped others, both individuals and units/organizations, find their way too.

The Rock—that would be the way my wife, Christine, and my children would describe me. Interestingly, no fewer than three different generals under whom I served also used "the rock" to describe me. They said it was the manner by which I carried out my role and what I meant to that organization.

Embolden—I was physically bullied at school, in part because I was dyslexic and overweight, and verbally bullied for much of my early life. My decision to join the military was the first step towards redressing that. I didn't just join the regular military, I joined the physically most difficult organization to get into, the Royal Marine Commandos. I did the commando course twice, first as a recruit, then two years later as an officer. After four years, I was selected for the Special Boat Service [the UK's equivalent of the US Navy SEALs]. *Embolden* is about giving others the strength and courage to be who they truly are and not what they might need to be to impress others or prevent themselves from being bullied.

You could say the David's purpose statement has more of those HR-like words in it than some of the others. It does, but when you drop into why those words matter, you step into a very powerful and rich set of life experiences that the words represent. Every time I have heard David describe his why, I feel I am being let into a sacred place, his purpose.

These examples were meant to help you expand the range of options of how you might articulate your own purpose statement. All the purpose statements we have reviewed have a set of common characteristics. Each purpose statement does the following:

1. Captures the unique gift you bring to the world
2. Springs from your own life experience (magical childhood moments, crucibles, passions)
3. Leverages words/symbols that have deep meaning for you
4. Uses a minimal number of words/symbols
5. Gives you access to that room of purpose that is yours only, each time you repeat it

Now it's your turn.

Defining your purpose

What follows is a five-step process designed to help you access your purpose statement. Each of us has a preferred approach to doing a reflective exercise of this type. I find writing by hand on a notepad helpful; for others, anything with a keyboard to type is where the deeper thoughts are discovered. Whichever you prefer is fine. What is more important is giving yourself the time to just think. Plane flights have been some of my favorite "thinking" places.

I promise you that the more you put into this exercise, the more what will speak back to you will be your purpose. If you have been answering the questions at the end of each chapter, great—you've got a head start. If not, let's get started.

Step 1: Childhood Magical Moments

For some of us, it is easy to reenter these moments. Personally, it took many years before I could access any magical moments. If they are there, proceed. If not, move to step 2. While you may have reflected on the questions at the end of chapter 3, take a moment to write even more details about what was happening in those moments.

1. When you were a kid, what activity or moment brought you the most joy and satisfaction? (This could be one specific moment, a specific activity, or a list of experiences.)
2. Write about one of those moments in vivid detail. Write about it as if you were back in the experience right now. You may want to include
   a. Who else, if anyone, was involved
   b. What time of year and time of day it was
   c. The sounds, smells, tastes that are part of this experience
   d. How you were feeling

As much as possible, we want you to be 100 percent back in that moment, experiencing it fully. The more you write, the better.

3. What are the key elements of the story that stand out? Jot them down.
4. Write down the key emotions this story evokes in you.

Step 2: Crucible Stories

For some of us (including me), our purpose shows itself in our most challenging experiences. By looking at these experiences in our lives, we can uncover the unique way we overcame the difficulties we faced. While you may have reflected on the questions at the end of chapter 4, take a moment to write even more details about those moments that shaped you.

1. Describe two or three of your most challenging life experiences—either personal or professional moments where you were tested the most. Here are a couple of guidelines:
    • Pick experiences that occurred in the past and are not currently impacting you. They have a beginning (things were fine), a middle (challenging events), and an end (things are back to normal or better now).
    • Keep writing until the story has a light at the end of the tunnel.
2. Write down what within you was key to getting through these experiences.
3. Clarify the gifts that these experiences bring to who you are as a leader.

Step 3: Passions in One's Life

Each of us has a set of activities that bring a deeper sense of joy and satisfaction and reconnect us to a part of ourself that is as essential as breathing. As we discussed in the last chapter, we approach these activities differently. What might be seen as a chore to others is seen as a set of activities that bring us a deep sense of vitality and aliveness. While you may have reflected on the questions in the last chapter, take a moment now to write even more details about the passion or passions that have been with you over time.

1. As you look at your journey in life, think of the activities and interests that have stayed with you over time. Just as our purpose never runs away, these passions are part of who we are. These activities may have no redeeming quality other than that we love doing them. They aren't even necessarily things we are good at. What is your passion?
2. Describe a particular moment when you were fully experiencing your passion.
3. Describe two other moments when you were fully experiencing your passion.
4. How do you feel in these moments?
5. Who are you in these moments?

Step 4: Accessing the Room of Purpose

I promise you will gain access to the room of purpose. What does that mean? Each of us has a place within us where we are energized, we have a twinkle (literally) in our eye, and the unique gift that we are—our purpose—is fully present. We may not know exactly how we got into this room but it's a really great place to be. Each of us has stepped into this room many times over our lifetime. Those who are fully leading from their purpose operate from this room much of the time. The more time we spend in it, the easier it is to realize when we are not there.

Our goal is to look across many experiences, so we can see the pattern.

1. As you read through your answers to the questions in steps 1 through 3, what makes you smile the most?
2. Write down the words that are connected to that smile.

Step 5: Your Purpose Statement: Finding the Thread of Purpose

Using what you now know, let's craft your purpose statement:

1. Stringing together the key words you captured in step 4, let's take a first cut at your purpose statement.

    The purpose that is leading me is: _____

    _____

2. At this point you may have it figured out or you may have four or five words that really are important, but the actual sentence isn't clear. Don't worry. Let's take the next step.

    Describe why each key word really matters to you: ____

    _____

3. Looking at what you have written, notice if a set of words appears that better defines your purpose. If so, write them down.

    The purpose that is leading me is: _____

    _____

If you have found the words that really make you smile, congratulations. If you are still playing with it, give it some time. One optional and powerful step remains for those of you who wish to enlist people around you in understanding the purpose that has been leading you.

Optional Step: Interviewing People around You

Whether or not you are still struggling with your purpose statement, this exercise will help. The people closest to you have deep insights about the unique gift that you bring to the world. As simple as this step seems, it has the power to have the greatest impact. Those who work with you—family members, mentors, and participants in previous adventures who value who you are—can speak to the gift you bring. This is what you should ask your spouse, friends, and people you currently work with:

1. If I disappeared tomorrow and was replaced with someone just as talented, what would you most miss?
2. What do you believe is my unique contribution to what we have done together?

Ask those you have worked with in the past or friends you haven't seen for a while these questions:

1. What do you most miss about what I brought to our adventures together?
2. What do you believe is my unique contribution to what we have done together?

Write down the common themes. Compare these themes to the words you wrote in step 5. Make any adjustments to your purpose statement and remember, what matters most is being in the room of purpose. It's okay to continue to play with the words until it feels right. I have changed the words I use three times in the last 10 years. It's the same room, just a different key! Make any upgrades you want. Now it's time to put it away and read about others' journey with purpose.

PART III

IMPACT

Chapter 6

IMPACT: CLARITY, FOCUS, AND THE CONFIDENCE TO ACT

If you didn't know the purpose that leads you, what do you believe would not have happened or you would not have experienced?

As we shift our focus from understanding what purpose is to appreciating the impact of leading from purpose, let me share one of the biggest *aha!*s from the more than 75 interviews I have conducted for this book. When I first started asking the question at the top of this page, it was an add-on, something I asked just to satisfy my own curiosity. Yet it always gave people pause and their answers crystallized the long-term impact of purpose. Without fail, three words come up as what would be missed if they hadn't had purpose front and center: *clarity, focus,* and *confidence,* especially when the outcome of a decision or action was unknown.

It turns out that, no matter what the events or circumstances, people who have discovered and lead from their purpose experience a significant increase in their level of clarity of focus and confidence to act.

Let's connect again with Jacqui, whose story we shared in the chapter on crucibles. Her response to the question is this:

JACQUI—Through tenacity, create brilliance.

We would have gotten only some of the business results. I wouldn't have applied the clarity and focus needed, and that would have impacted our financial results. I made some clear decisions about key resources and determined to make sure that the 30-, 60-days' execution plan really was done right. I am far more confident about who I am.

We live in a world characterized by the *lack* of clarity, focus, and confidence. Even a mundane task can be challenging. Once, when my then 15-year-old daughter Renee asked me to pick up a box of Cheez-It crackers, I was glad to do something that wouldn't be received with a look of "I am so embarrassed to be around you, Dad." I thought it would be so easy.

Walking down the cracker aisle, I was stopped in my tracks by an unforeseen problem: 12 different Cheez-It varieties stared back at me. I felt my clarity and focus evaporate, and whatever confidence I had went right out the window when the simple act of buying Cheez-Its turned into a choice among multiple varieties. After about five minutes, I found a box of basic Cheez-Its on the bottom shelf and grabbed it! (Note that there are now 32 varieties; faced with that, I might never have made it home from the store.)

My Cheez-It experience is a humorous, maybe even a silly, example of our world in which the options thrown at us range from usually inconsequential day-to-day choices to what profession to choose, job to take, or actions to execute. Unlike selecting crackers, many of these choices have profound impacts over time. Purpose can lead us and help us make these decisions by bringing us to a place of clarity, focus, and confidence, especially when the territory we need to travel is unknown to us.

What does it mean to have clarity, be able to focus, and experience the confidence to act? What do these words really mean? Let's start with clarity.

Clarity

clar·i·ty
ˈklerədē
noun
Oxford English Dictionary: **the quality of being certain or definite**: *it was clarity of purpose that he needed.*

The *Oxford English Dictionary* example that connects clarity with purpose makes me smile. I have seen this phenomenon before in many forms:

MIGUEL—To be the captain of storytelling that lights people up.

If I didn't know my purpose, I wouldn't be in my current role, that is for sure. Until I understood my purpose, I wasn't clear. I was drifting through life without a plan.

When I started leading from my purpose, it was like a veil had been lifted. It's a surreal experience. It clarifies so many aspects of who I am. Once you see the jigsaw puzzle the picture makes sense. You have so much more clarity as to what you want to do next. I now know what I am really here for.

When purpose is leading us, we experience greater clarity about who we are and what really matters. Probably the biggest decision we each make with no reliable knowledge of the outcome is which career, role, or job we will pursue. Any information provided before we make our move is always far thinner than the reality we find. So many leaders tell me about taking a role or job that was the biggest mistake of their life. They all knew in their heart of hearts that they were not meant to stay, yet they usually stayed far longer than was good for anyone involved. In giving us access to our deepest heart of hearts, purpose turns out to be a great provider of clarity. For example, Dolf (whom we will hear from again) explains it this way:

DOLF—Be the gardener with boundless curious energy to grow a better world.

Knowing my purpose makes very clear what I *don't* want. It shifts things from something you feel in your stomach to something you talk about. I don't want to be head of mergers and acquisitions. What I am drawn to is leading a group of people who have a really big challenge and want to grow. The edge is now putting my purpose at the service of having a bigger impact, the wider community.

Many executives will tell you that their career was just a series of fortunate opportunities. They simply took what was offered and kept going. How many of us are just drifting through life without a real plan? Are you where you are in your career because someone offered you a job and you took it, then you were offered the next opportunity, or because you knew what mattered to you and worked to make it happen? For each of us, our life energy—our most precious resource—has an unknown expiration date.

In chapter 1 we met Jostein Solheim, the CEO of Ben & Jerry's. His decision to stay in his current role instead of taking a promotion exemplifies this. Purpose provides the clarity that allows us to see what really matters to us. For Jostein it was to stay as CEO of Ben & Jerry's for the next five-plus years.

I had the clarity at that moment from the place of purpose that I had to own the legacy of Ben & Jerry's. I couldn't just be passing through anymore. I initiated a process in which we did a 10-year strategy on climate change and social justice that took 18 months to define. We call it "climate justice." Ben & Jerry's and the board were heavily involved, along with employees.

Clarity has always been in short supply. It is something we all wish for ourselves and from those we work with, yet it is so easily lost. Over the years, I have participated in many informal discussions about what is missing from senior management, and a good dose of clarity and focus is always on the list. Almost to a person, participants complain that "leading" with significant *un*clarity and lack of focus results in indecision and "politics as usual."

Focus

What happens when we add "focus"?

fo·cus

'fōkəs

verb

The Oxford English Dictionary: **adapt to the prevailing level of light and become able to see clearly.**

Notice that this definition takes the world around us into consideration. We are not immune to or magically protected from our environment. As the VUCA world accelerates, new players that didn't exist five years ago redefine industries, elections elevate individuals who would have been unimaginable in times gone by, and climate change forces us to rethink our day-to-day lives. We are deeply affected by the world.

Purpose will not protect you from what is happening, but it does help you "adapt to the prevailing level of light"—that is, the deeper truths about the world around us—and see clearly what others cannot. This is one of the greatest gifts of purpose and what leading from purpose is most able to provide: the ability to see clearly when the prevailing level of light is at best a cloudy day. Remember how Dirk explained the power of being focused when he told his story about finding the whistle in the dark forest:

DIRK—Race to the unknown—let's find the whistle!

Purpose allows you to actually be less reckless because you know that in one way or another you will get there. Do not rush. The longer you stay in the dark, the greater the likelihood for success. You have to be patient to be successful. The reward is bigger if you take your time and stay in the "unknown" for a bit.

Confidence

Confidence comes from a Latin word meaning to "have full trust." This captures what leaders tell me about the impact of purpose for them. They talk from a place of finally having full trust in themselves, a place that wasn't as accessible before. We can all recall moments in which we felt confident as well as those when we wished we did but actually didn't. Maybe we can fake it with others but, inside, we always know.

con·fi·dence

'känfədəns

noun

Merriam-Webster's Dictionary: **faith or belief that one will act in a right, proper, or effective way.**

Confidence is not the same as *certainty*. In fact, we most need confidence in situations in which the outcome is unknown. Confidence doesn't give us the power to be all-knowing and infallible.

We find another common misuse of *confidence* in performance reviews, as in, "Jeff needs to show greater confidence by being more demanding of his direct reports as well as more outspoken in senior team meetings." Really, is *this* the definition of a good leader? I do not believe that having confidence is in any way equated with a particular leadership style. When people say they want someone to be more confident, they are usually saying they want him or her to be more extroverted and directive. That may be how they should behave, but *style* is the issue here, not confidence. No one style is perfect for all situations, and, as we will see, purpose gives us the latitude—and the confidence—to lead from multiple styles.

What is important is that each of us needs to have faith or believe that what we are doing and where we are leading others is the right, proper, or effective path. Much of what leaders do is to help those around them to have the faith or belief they need in order to act.

Sometimes just having the belief that we can act in an effective way in the face of an unknown challenge is half the battle. The story we tell ourselves can matter as much as the events around us. Christina Habib, who shared her magical moment story about kites and rockets, says it well.

CHRISTINA—To catalyze people who fly a kite to build the rocket.

Leading from my purpose helps me access the confidence to step out of my comfort zone. It originates from an "authentic" belief that anything can be better than it was before. The confidence I gain helps others overcome their own demons and bring their purpose out. It brings a sense of community and clarity. I am not superhuman. We are all incomplete and balance each other out. What's funny is my confidence has an interesting impact for those who want to just fly a kite, when they realize that I am about rockets!

Purpose's most ubiquitous gift is a huge dose of clarity of focus and confidence—these are the qualities we wish for most, especially when we lead, or others lead us. It is no coincidence that people who have connected to their purpose experience higher levels of these attributes. For years, I have explained purpose as being a unique set of glasses that lets us see what others cannot. My *aha!* moment came from putting two and two together and seeing the alignment: Put on your glasses, which allow you to *focus* and have the *clarity* that gives you the *confidence* to take actions aligned with your purpose.

In the remainder of the book, we go on a great journey, exploring the full impact of leading from purpose. Clarity, focus, and confidence are so pervasive that every chapter could be labeled "clarity of focus and the confidence to act," but I have much more to share with you. Each aspect deserves its own voice. Here is what we will discover.

Growth you can count on

Living and leading from purpose have the potential to transform organizations and produce miraculous business growth. The key is what is known as the "growth mindset." This is the belief that our intelligence and capabilities are not stagnant, as they are with a "fixed mindset," but instead continue to adapt and develop as we apply ourselves. If you access your purpose you access the growth mindset, deepening, in turn, your connection to your purpose. When we apply this gift of purpose to work, we see the sort of business growth that all businesses desire.

The Key to Authenticity

One of the gifts of purpose is that it allows us to connect the events of our past to who we are now, and who we are becoming. Through our purpose, we see our journey through time and can confidently step into our authentic selves. Purpose isn't just another element of authentic leadership; it is the path to it.

Standing on Solid Ground

Your purpose is not attached to one profession, expertise, or role; it is a constant. If we commit ourselves to stepping into purpose, we find that our roles no longer define us. Our identity becomes centered from our purpose.

The True Source of Energy

When we have energy, we can deal with anything; when we're drained, leading gets hard and leading authentically gets harder. Understand how purpose is at the root of what energizes us.

Stress That's Good for You

Purpose changes our relationship to stress and can help us transform a "threat response" into a "challenge response." This shift allows us to rise to the occasion, increase our self-confidence, and step into the room of purpose.

Choosing the Hard Right over the Easy Wrong

Our purpose is what points us toward a deeper truth. True leading is about going where no one else has gone. Knowing our purpose gives us the ability to see the reality of our options more clearly, and that, in turn, gives us the courage to choose the hard right over the easy wrong.

Purpose and Happiness

Pursuing happiness for the sake of happiness is about feeling good in the present. Living from purpose allows us to integrate the past, present, and future, and see the deeper meaning of the path we are on.

Saving the World, Saving Yourself

We see the echo of our purpose in those we help or serve. Yet, it is only when we apply our purpose to ourselves that we finally come home and become able to lead from our purpose at the most compelling level of congruency. You can't save the world if you don't take care of yourself first. Purpose will help you do that if you let it.

Getting Organizational Purpose to Work

When a leader's purpose aligns with his or her organization's, magic happens. The gauntlet that tests this alignment is fierce, and the negative impact of incongruence is humbling. We will look at the four key elements to making it all work.

Mastery in the Room of Purpose

Are you in the room of purpose, or are you one of those "cold and timid souls who neither know victory nor defeat"? It's a powerful question that captures the reality of leading from purpose. Many of us answer *yes*, we want to lead from our purpose. Yet for those of us—including myself—whose stories you have read in these pages, the fact is that our purpose is always there waiting for us. The challenge is to fully listen. In this final chapter we uncover the secret to true mastery.

Let's start now, with growth you can count on.

Chapter 7

IMPACT: GROWTH YOU CAN COUNT ON

I was called by another company to be CEO. I saw
they really weren't ready to grow at the level I knew
was possible and I said no. I won't do that job...it isn't
aligned with my purpose.

—Pablo

Everyone thought I was mad, from single- to double-digit
growth and we achieved it. The key is creating stretch
ambitions that are not so mad that people write it off
but enough to energize people and think differently
about what they have to do.

—Jan

I have collected many stories of magical business growth that are
associated with a leader's clarity of purpose. It does happen—
and surprisingly often—but the numbers are not the measure of
real growth. Real growth you can count on is what happens on
the inside. Still, positive results tend to show up as a side effect
of leading from purpose. Let's begin with a few examples of just
that: business growth and lots of it, in ways others didn't think
possible or likely. These individuals each brought their unique

gift that made the difference. Then we will look at the real growth you can count on that really matters.

Improving lives and the bottom line

EHSAN—To improve the life of the common man.

Ehsan Malik has a purpose that seems simple, yet he has had a huge impact on many people in Pakistan. His purpose statement is *"To improve the life of the common man."* In 2006, he became the head of Unilever Pakistan. That period was right in the middle of some of the most difficult times of the war with the Taliban insurgency in that region of the world. From 2006 to 2016, Ehsan grew the business by 400 percent, with profits increasing 500 percent.

When Ehsan took the job, he looked at it from the perspective of his purpose. The common man had little access to the products he sold. In Pakistan in 2006, one child in 10 died before the age of five. At the most basic level, providing soap to children to wash their hands daily had a direct impact by reducing childhood deaths from common illnesses. At the other end of the income spectrum, most of us take shampoo for granted. In rural Pakistan, washing hair with simple soap was the norm; just try using bar soap as shampoo for one day and see how your hair feels. In the Pakistan of 2006, all the products Ehsan sold sat in stores in the big cities.

Ehsan wasn't thinking about business growth. He was thinking about how to reach people in rural areas to help them live a better life. Today, Unilever's Sustainable Living Plan includes doing just that, around the globe, but that plan wouldn't exist for another three years and Ehsan wasn't the kind of guy who waits.

Ehsan transformed the business from serving about 100,000 shops to serving over 300,000, with most of the increase in places where no soap or shampoo had ever been sold. He created a whole campaign to help people in remote parts of Pakistan understand the benefit of using shampoo instead of coarse soap to wash their hair. People became so excited—their hair was so much softer than they had ever experienced. He strongly supported his team's idea of communicating the health benefits of regular use of soap as a basic means of health and hygiene for children. He invested in educating mothers about the health benefits of using soap regularly. In some villages, the local doctors were up in arms a year after he introduced Lifebuoy soap: They had fewer patients because kids weren't getting sick! For Ehsan, this was his purpose speaking to him. The "common man" was the kids who didn't get sick, the woman whose hair felt soft, and the men who proudly ran a shop that sold consumer goods and could successfully raise a family.

After a great year, the team wanted to celebrate with an off-site team-building meeting. They pushed hard to go to a luxury resort as their reward. Ehsan laughed and told them to go deep into rural Pakistan and live with a poor consumer for a week. Go visit the real people and live in their houses and see what they do when they wake up. Do they brush their teeth? How do they preserve the milk from their cow? "What do they do in their lives and how can we help them?" was his call to action. If you repeat asking a team to go live with a poor family by a thousand little moments like that over 10 years, you achieve great business impact. You also end up with the most women in senior leadership roles in a large multinational in Pakistan. (Both Ehsan's predecessor and his successor were women, as were most members of the management committee.) Indeed, this purpose-led approach to improving the lives of common people resulted in Unilever Pakistan training and empowering thousands of women entrepreneurs in villages to promote its products through home-based salons. These women in turn directed a major part of their earnings toward educating themselves and their siblings, caring for elderly parents, and improving their homes. It's a great example of one purpose-led action having multiple positive effects in the community.

Ehsan completely understood that without his purpose he would have been a lost soul. It would have been so easy to do his job without focusing on benefiting the common man. He could have gone head-to-head with his competitors in the big cities and grown at a healthy 10 percent—and been miserable in the end. The growth he was looking for was not just the numbers that everyone else was chasing. His growth was the growth of Pakistan as a country and its people. That's how you get your 400 percent.

Growth with tenacity and brilliance

In chapter 4, Jacqui showed us how our crucible stories can be a powerful access point to purpose. What do we get if we apply Jacqui's purpose, "Through tenacity, deliver brilliance," to the metrics of revenue and business performance? To find out, I went back to Jacqui and asked her that question. I wanted to understand her answer because the stories she shared in chapter 4 are all about thriving in chaos with no clear upside.

JACQUI—Through tenacity, deliver brilliance.

In 2012, Jacqui decided to put herself to the test by taking a job as the New Zealand country manager for a large home improvement retailer. When she called a friend with the good news, her friend laughed, "What the hell do you know about timber?" At that moment, not one thing.

The company had acquired the number-three home improvement retailer in New Zealand in 2002, but the initial enthusiasm was quickly replaced by reality. In Australia, her organization is synonymous with home improvement, but the chain didn't have that image in New Zealand. The competition was smart, nimble, and well established. Over 10 years of hard work, Rod, Jacqui's predecessor, had grown the business to around half a billion ($NZ) in sales. It had been a hard fight with nowhere near the results they had hoped for. The Australian business, on the other hand, was big and sexy—the darling of the retail industry, with new stores opening every two weeks. Jacqui was stepping into the shoes of someone the employees thought of as a lifetime home improvement guru. Rod was heading back to Australia to a significant and well-deserved promotion.

Jacqui was never going to be Rod or wield a power tool with precision. Her new boss had hired her because he wanted to create a step change in the business and intuitively felt she had what was needed. The question was, did she or didn't she?

Let's look at her purpose. "Through tenacity, deliver brilliance." How does "through tenacity" suggest that she would approach her role? Jacqui's way is not to make big strategic plays of acquisitions or huge financial investments in new stores. Instead, she focused on the details. She spent months going to the stores and talking with everyone—her team, store employees, customers. She put on a green apron and worked alongside the store teams. What did they do when a customer was upset? How did they address an out-of-stock item? She began to see which functions, stores, and groups were well aligned, and which ones needed to up their game. She began to see who was or wasn't able to step up.

In some meetings, she saw people who were oblivious to the critical problems staring them in the face and to the changes that needed to be made. They didn't have the tenacity Jacqui knew was necessary to totally transform a basic retail business. She realized that she needed to get everyone across the board to operate at a much more responsive pace.

She jumped right into everything from the beginning, mapping out which functions to focus on first. She had tough discussions, helping function heads who rose to the challenge and replacing those who didn't. People began to feel a jolt of energy and excitement about where the business was going. They all knew the score and what was being asked of them. "Right leaders with the right expectations create right results" was the phrase she lived by. By the end of 2012, the business was starting to show same-store increases of 4 to 6 percent.

Jacqui focused on all the little things—positive actions that are contagious and create an upward spiral. She noticed that, except for the color of the building, the stores looked and felt just like the competition. Same products, same service, same everything. Instead of big splashy changes or a big push to open lots of stores, she chose to create a different experience for the customer—brighter, cleaner, and much friendlier.

As Jacqui upgraded the senior leadership team, she continued to spend time in the stores. Today she figures she has met at least 85 percent of the more than 4,000 employees through barbecue breakfasts, dunking the boss (they love that one), and working alongside them.

Existing store sales climbed, and the increase has stayed constant at 8 percent for the last four years. The footprint of 47 stores did increase to 54, yet the sales revenue doubled to $1 billion (NZ). All from having the tenacity to work through every function and every store in creating an experience for customers that is friendlier, brighter, and cleaner than any competitor in the market.

> Part of the drive of change is letting people know where they are and the openness....Transparency. How you deliver the result. *Deliver brilliance* is about how it feels. That is what my purpose does for me...financials, interactions, in every moment. I have leveraged my purpose through everything I do. My purpose linked everything together. I now drive things harder in the right way. Tenacity and brilliance are one and the same for me.

Jacqui has a daily practice. At the end of each day she reflects on how well she has lived her purpose. When she realizes she didn't fully live it in a particular moment or situation, she goes back the next day and does it right.

If you run a business, you know that having a couple of quarters or two years of growth is challenging but not what really matters. Getting short-term growth is great, but what is hardest to get, and what matters most, is continued growth over time. Jacqui's purpose is perfectly designed for just that. (Speaking of continued growth, remember that one of Jacqui's crucible stories was about being homeless with a newborn child and two small children. She is now a proud grandmother with 10 grandchildren!)

When Jacqui read these pages, she asked me to add all the things the team did to get the results. True, each person contributed their unique gift to what became a great success story. Yet the question is, *what wouldn't happen if we weren't there?* If you ask Jacqui's team that question, they will tell you that "Ms. Tenacity and Brilliance" brought something special that created real growth you can count on.

Real growth you can count on

What can we learn from these examples of fiscal growth? Neither Ehsan nor Jacqui were preoccupied with the numbers. Each was dramatically innovative and creative in his or her domain. They faced considerable challenges externally and substantial amounts of disbelief and resistance within the organizations they served.

The purpose that leads you most likely doesn't have the word *growth* as a key ingredient; in my experience, only one in a hundred do. Still, many people we work with have been astounded by the level of business growth they have experienced after discovering their purposes. I have had the opportunity to review thousands of self-assessments of executives who defined their purpose in our programs and then created plans describing how they were going to lead from their purpose. The thing I hear most often is, "I was too conservative in the goals I set when I wrote this."

One way to explain purpose and its impact on growth is to look at the work of Carol Dweck. In her landmark book *Mindset*, she defines what she calls the "growth mindset." According to her research, we all tend to look at the world in one of two ways: with a *growth* or a *fixed* mindset. In the growth mindset, we believe that our intelligence and capabilities develop when we apply ourselves. In the fixed mindset, we believe we have a fixed level of intelligence and capabilities. We have all met people who believe that they are who they are, take it or leave it. What you see is what you get. Surprisingly, when we praise our kids and tell them that they are naturally gifted, we reinforce the fixed mindset. They leave saying, "I am good at *a*, *b*, or *c*." When we validate the actual hard *effort* they put in to getting the desired outcome, we strengthen the growth mindset. They think, "I can learn *x*, *y*, or *z* if I really apply myself."

Carol Dweck's research shows us that students who believe their intelligence is fixed will structure their lives to validate being smart by taking courses that don't challenge their view of themselves. This shapes every aspect of their lives, including the friends they pick and the activities they pursue. They will abandon a friendship when there is conflict or stress instead of working harder to get to the other side. On the other hand, students with a growth mindset see that with effort they can dramatically improve their level of intelligence, capabilities, and ability to be effective in the world. They spend less time convincing the world they are smart and more time developing their smartness. Difficulties are viewed as opportunities to grow, not situations to run away from. The difference boils down to this: those with a fixed mindset are more focused on being popular and avoiding rejection than on taking any risks.

Heidi Grant-Halvorson, in *Succeed*, an excellent summary of the research into what makes us succeed, captures Carol Dweck's work with this example: "On Valentine's Day, these children would make valentines for the most popular children, hoping to win their favor. Those more focused on avoiding rejection would make valentines only for the children who they knew would give one in return. On the other hand, the children who believed they could improve and grow as a person tended to choose goals that were more about developing relationships. Their valentines went to children they said they would like to know better, opening the door to friendship."

As interesting as this might be, you are probably wondering what this has to do with purpose. It turns out there is no more powerful and effective means to turn on the growth mindset than discovering and living from purpose. I have seen brittle senior leaders who are the definition of the fixed mindset turn their lives around after making this connection. Their purpose redefines their relationship to their work. The consistent theme from across all the interviews we have conducted is that purpose demands a growth mindset. If you access your purpose you access the growth mindset, deepening in turn your connection to your purpose.

- Purpose always wakes you up to the next thing you need to step into.
- You can achieve a goal, but your purpose will always show you the next door.
- Purpose defines the core essence of who you are, not where you end up.
- Instead of a place to get to, it's a journey to be on.
- It's okay to fall off the path because it's not going anywhere. You get up, and once you are back on it, you know it.

How the growth mindset works with purpose

PHILIPPE—To be an inquisitive actor who stages new worlds.

From the growth mindset perspective, let's take a look at Philippe. I can't think of a better example of a purpose that generates a growth mindset in all aspects of one's life.

Philippe's purpose statement is *"To be an inquisitive actor who stages new worlds."* The word "inquisitive" relates to his abundance of curiosity—he can't help but ask the questions no one else is asking. The word "actor" is about taking action (as opposed to being passive) as well as bringing artistic elements to his impact in the world. "Stages new worlds" means that it's not just about asking questions but creating new businesses and platforms in the real world. It can be big or small, and it's about contributing rather than having a particular job or title. "Business as usual" is like death to him—he feels alive when he is creating or identifying something that isn't the usual and that makes a difference.

Philippe's first job was with IBM. He was hired into marketing but wanted to be in sales. His boss said that wasn't possible, but he persisted—staging new worlds doesn't get handed to you on a plate. He was finally given six mothballed accounts that nobody wanted to deal with, the ones that all others had failed to get back, the ones that had been written off. The lens of purpose is an interesting thing. When you are the inquisitive actor staging new worlds, you look at a situation from a broader context. As he looked at each of these six accounts and the history of what had been done, Philippe realized that nobody had looked at the bigger picture. Talking with the clients, he asked questions and discussed strategic issues that no IBM sales guy these clients had ever met had done. Over time he re-signed all six accounts, created $14 million in new sales, and reopened a distribution network of about 500 new outlets selling IBM consumer products again, earning him an award for the best new business results achieved in his European division.

Next Philippe went to Motorola, where he staged new worlds by starting a division in the French market. Once again, the inquisitive actor was at play. By just asking questions of potential clients he turned a quick $15 million in incremental sales and, most importantly, created a brand-new distribution network of 1,500 point-of-sales, giving him and his team the best performance across the region for similar new divisions. It was so successful that Motorola decided to reintegrate the business back into the mainstream organization. The message was, "Great job; now just be a regular guy and work like everyone else." This was painful for Philippe. In some ways, this is a perfect example of the fixed mindset versus the growth mindset in an organization. Taking this role would have moved Philippe away from embarking on new journeys and staging something new. "I felt like I was going to die. I said no to the job. I became more aware of what my purpose was at that moment."

For some of us the growth mindset gets more activated as we become clear about our purpose. In all my interviews, I have never heard a story about going from the growth to the fixed mindset as an expression of purpose.

Philippe can't help it. Whenever he takes a new job he sees things through the lens of questioning what we do and why we do it. Others see him as highly creative, yet he feels he is just asking questions others don't think to ask. "I ask very simple questions; my mindset leads me to redefine the job that I was supposed to be doing. It redefines the business I am working in."

Philippe decided to put a purple cow on his phone. For Philippe, Seth Godin's book *Purple Cow* (a great read) is about the fact that most of what people do and create looks like just another cow in a field of cows. What would happen if there really *was* a purple cow? Then what? His team's mantra is "Let's go find the purple cow!"

"If I don't really grow I feel unhappy, so I do stuff in multiple worlds—work isn't the only stage." As for many of us, there are times when work doesn't give Philippe the stage he would like to have to bring his gifts. We lead from our purpose in all parts of our life.

Bringing the growth mindset to personal life

Many of us have been and will always be effective at operating from our purpose in our work, whether we know our purpose statement or not. Many of us need to step into the growth mind-set in how we bring our purpose to our personal lives. Getting clarity of purpose was extremely helpful to Philippe's relationship with his daughter. "I am growing and living my purpose with the ones I care about…new stages of the world that really matter for me. This has been one of the biggest differences now that I know my purpose. I now spend three hours a week trying to create a new world for my daughter as a short story. What is more impor-tant than bringing our unique purpose to our children?"

Growth all around

I hope these stories have expanded your view of what growth means in relationship to purpose. Yes, purpose is a powerful catalyst for improved financial performance. If you remem-ber, in chapter 1 we saw Jostein Solheim of Ben & Jerry's take the business from single-digit decline to double-digit growth while leading from his purpose. In this chapter, we introduced you to Ehsan and showed you the business impact of Jacqui and Philippe's purpose. Yet purpose is so much bigger than the num-bers. Purpose is about who you are as you get the numbers. The gift of the growth mindset is that it prompts us to lead a life that brings the curious kid inside of us into the game. We step into a level of curiosity and adventure that changes the experience, not only for us but also for all the people we lead.

Points to ponder

1. What is your best story of having participated in creating powerful business results?

2. During that experience, were you operating from the growth or the fixed mindset?
3. At this moment in time, where in your professional life are you operating from a growth mindset?
4. At this moment in time, where in your professional life are you operating from a fixed mindset?
5. What would be the upside of shifting even more to the growth mindset both at work and at home?

Chapter 8

IMPACT: THE KEY TO AUTHENTICITY

> Purpose defines the unique gifts people bring to leadership challenges, through which they can align others with their purposes in order to create positive impact. This is far more important than focusing entirely on achieving success in metrics like money, fame and power, yet ultimately produces sustained success in those metrics as well.
>
> —Bill George

I have spent the last decade collaborating with Bill George and it's had a significant impact on my understanding of what it means to be an authentic leader and determining the essence of purpose. Webster defines *authentic* as "real or genuine; not copied or false; true and accurate." It comes from the Greek word for *author*. At the core of authenticity is that place of authorship. Can you author your leadership and your life without knowing your purpose? I don't believe so, and Bill is the one who has kept challenging me to deepen our joint understanding of the impact of purpose on leadership.

Bill's words above, from one of his more recent articles, capture much of what we have discovered. Money, fame, and power are interesting bedfellows in life, yet going for them directly tends not to create the positive impact we all desire. Purpose provides a foundation that allows alignment with the purposes of others to create an outcome that also may bring fame and fortune.

Bill's first book, *Authentic Leadership*, follows his own journey to authenticity as a leader and offers his insights on what it means to be an authentic leader. With transparency and vulnerability, he shares his trials, wake-up calls, and challenging life experiences as a highly visible CEO and board member of two *Fortune* 50 companies. Bill was the first nonacademic to write about authentic leadership. Academics describe authentic leadership from the outside in, but Bill has lived it from the inside. Here is a bit of his journey in his own words:

Hitting the Wall

"In the middle of the road of my life, I awoke in a dark wood, where the true way was wholly lost," Dante writes in *The Divine Comedy*. My most agonizing time in the career crucible also came when I least expected it. I call this "hitting the wall," something that happens to most leaders at least once in their careers. As painful as it was, this experience provided the basis for growth and change that transformed my career. It caused me to look inside myself, acknowledge my shortcomings, and realize I was on the wrong path....

Honeywell. What began as a huge promotion turned into a decision to reassess my career and to move in an entirely new direction....During this period I started questioning whether Honeywell was really the place for me. I have always seen myself as a growth-oriented leader, not a turnaround specialist.... I also found myself becoming more concerned with appearances and my attire than with being myself. Reluctantly, I faced up to the reality that Honeywell was changing me more than I was changing it. I had "hit the wall," but was too proud to face it. I felt I was in a trap from which I couldn't escape.

The macho side of me said, "I have to tough it out." Sure, I was leading, but the purpose of my efforts was not at all clear. Where was my "leading" leading to?... Like Dante, I too was "in a dark wood."

Bill is asking the most basic question that we are attempting to answer in this book. Where is your "leading" leading to? When our purpose isn't clear, as in that moment it wasn't for Bill, we can feel lost, as he so eloquently describes. Fortunately, he didn't stay lost and instead this moment became a wake-up call. In the end, he stepped into the COO role at Medtronic, a very small company in comparison to Honeywell. Yet within Medtronic he thrived, eventually becoming CEO and growing the business so successfully over a 10-year period that the stock value increased from $1 billion to $60 billion. At the peak of his career, he left the corporate world to become an academic. Later I asked him what motivated him to start a new career in his late fifties; his answer is a good indication of the quality of leader he has become: He was disappointed by his generation of leaders and felt a need to ensure that we find a better way. In 2004, Bill was invited to teach his approach to authentic leadership at Harvard Business School.

When Bill and I met in 2006, we already shared a deep

understanding of each of the key elements of the approach, from the power of unpacking crucible stories to the importance of clarifying values. We knew that purpose was important, yet we didn't fully understand the role it plays.

Purpose's gift to authenticity

When I first started teaching authentic leadership to executives, I was willing to leave purpose out of the equation—until I noticed the difference between programs that included purpose and those that didn't. In all our programs, participants tell deep and powerful stories from their lives—stories of loss, difficulty, and perseverance as well as stories of wild success and validation. Participants begin to "see" who they have been most of their lives. Their values, strengths, motivations, weaknesses, and lifelong patterns become clear.

Yet when I left purpose out of a program, these moments of deep insight led some participants to stand up with great satisfaction and say things like, "I am a straight-shooting, take-no-prisoners leader. I can now ignore all the feedback I got suggesting I should change," or, "I am a quiet, reserved person, and this is just who I am." People were confusing a *style preference* that showed up as a pattern in their stories with the core of who they were.

We all have styles of operating that are more comfortable, ways of seeing the world, and life experiences that have shaped us.

good cop versus bad cop

conservative versus liberal

childhood divorce versus picture-perfect childhood

We have developed preferred styles of interacting with the

world as a result. Yet, I have watched "authenticity" be used as a shield, ironically protecting us from a journey to a deeper sense of who we are as a leader and as a person, when purpose is left out of consideration.

We all know people who are one-trick ponies. They have one predominant style of dealing with the world. Learning new ways of operating just isn't part of their playbook. They may think they are authentic, but being led by them is usually the very definition of inauthenticity. They "are who they are" (their style), and you must adapt accordingly. It can be appealing from afar, but it is not satisfying up close.

In chapter 7, I introduced Carol Dweck's concept of fixed mindset versus growth mindset. Fixed mindset is the one-trick pony approach to life. The goal is to find situations that validate your view of yourself, allowing you to succeed using your "trick" and not surprising you with experiences that test your style.

Purpose pivots us toward the growth mindset. Instead of having one style to be validated through one's stories, the discussion is about a journey, always stepping into a fuller version of purpose. Just as we must not let our role, job, or expertise define us, we must not allow ourselves to believe our authenticity is dependent on doing things the way we like to do them. This is what happens when we believe that we *are* our style.

True, trying new things can be awkward. When we step into new situations and are stretched, we feel and may even appear less authentic in the short term. However, if we see ourselves as our purpose instead of defining ourselves by our style, we are more willing to stretch and take risks. Most new jobs come with both the tasks we like doing and are already good at (what we were hired for), and all the new responsibilities that feel foreign, ranging from developmental challenges to the way meetings are run to how we fill out our expense reports. Yet, over time all these became natural and our feeling and appearance of authenticity recover.

Of course, we each have a preferred style of how we want to interact with the world. But isn't it funny how many of our most challenging experiences end up being situations in which our style meets the world and the world runs right over us? It may be difficult in the short term, but when we are forced to dig deeper and find solid ground, with luck, we end up operating more from purpose and find we have multiple styles available to us. When did you have the greatest growth and development in your life? Was it when your style was your answer to every question, or was it when you were put in situations that demanded you stretch and integrate multiple styles?

You might say that you are direct—"What you see is what you get"—and always telling people the truth. But that is a style of leading, not who you are. Any style taken to its extreme will get us in trouble. The research on what causes high-flying leaders to fail proves the point. They fail not because of their weaknesses, but because they overuse a style or strength: being too results-oriented and not focusing on the bigger picture, being too confrontational and not building trusting relationships, or being too relationship-focused and unable to make hard people decisions. When we confuse our style with who we are, we become more inauthentic.

Purpose sits underneath all our styles and allows us to access a deeper level of authenticity. If you are your style, how unique

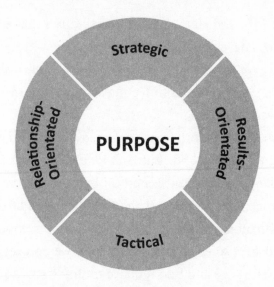

and authentic are you really? What better way to author yourself than to access your purpose?

Accessing other styles of leading from the foundation of purpose

ANNA—Inspire others to take a chance and own the stage.

What happens when a New York corporate lawyer discovers purpose? Anna's purpose statement is "Inspire others to take a chance and own the stage." As a kid, she loved to perform and was involved in many musicals as she grew up. On stage, she felt she could be anyone she wanted to be. She could have a voice and give a message that helped you learn something new. She loved to push people to come out of their shell, to own their stage in life and be who they really wanted to be.

Yet, when I met Anna, I saw only the corporate lawyer who was highly focused and disciplined and knew her domain. I also experienced someone who seemed cautious. Anna was a good example of "staying in the box." Hers was a very effective corporate style; it just wasn't authentically Anna.

As she uncovered her purpose, it was as if she had stepped into a spotlight. When she stepped into her room of purpose, she felt she was back on stage with her authentic voice, only this time she no longer needed a musical to perform in. Her purpose became the stage from which she could express her voice.

Leading from purpose caused Anna to lead more authentically in some surprising ways. In the past, when the marketing team engaged with her, Anna would focus on the contract and look at the language. Now she asked the marketers for their vision, what would make them proud, and how they could make it better. She wanted them to think about what they were doing and leave a lasting impression. At first the marketing team was taken aback, but the outcome was a much better approach, in addition to a contract that worked.

In another situation, a team wanted to run a big customer event and presented several decisions for Anna's legal input. Handling the contracts would be easy, but first she had a set of questions for the team:

- How can we make this event legendary?
- How do we blow it out of the water with our limited funds?
- What is our social engagement and how will people remember us?
- Do participants have an opportunity to give back and make a difference in the world?

This is not your predictable cautious corporate lawyer. Anna was stepping into her purpose and finding the authentic leader who had always been there. As the organization began to realize that Anna had many talents, Karen, a relatively new senior executive, asked for her help with an important presentation. Anna helped Karen leverage her purpose by telling a story about sailing—one of Karen's passions connected to her purpose—as the start of her talk. It was a defining moment that allowed clients and senior executives to see *who* Karen was as opposed to *what* she was. Anna told me, "I combined my personal purpose with Karen's, allowing her to lead from her purpose."

Then, about six months later, Anna approached me with an interesting request. We often train internal alumni to take groups of participants through our purpose process. Most people who make this request are from HR. Corporate lawyer Anna asked to be trained.

I wasn't sure at first, but as Anna spoke about her experience of accessing her purpose, I began to see a part of her that I had not interacted with in the past. She was asking for a chance to build her skills, as her legal role didn't give her opportunities to experiment. She was looking for a way to stretch way beyond her comfortable, cautious style that had been highly effective as a senior legal counsel—it just wasn't truly Anna.

Each time Anna has facilitated a group over the past five years, she has shown stronger listening skills and ability to help others uncover what is hidden. Of course, just knowing her purpose has not magically given her easy access to a different style of leading. Her purpose was pushing her to step out of her comfort zone and connect to something deeper. Working with people from many different functions and levels has tested her. When I coach her, she always gives me a look of "Okay, let's see" and jumps right back in. Did it feel inauthentic in the moment when my suggestion was a stretch for her? Yes, absolutely. And Anna was digging for a deeper authenticity. But Anna knows that it's impossible to develop a range of styles if the old one is working just fine. So repeatedly she puts herself in situations way outside her traditional legal counsel role.

Through helping others feel comfortable telling their stories and sharing the meaning in their life, Anna's approach to managing meetings has completely changed. She now has new choices in her leadership style that go far beyond her former guarded approach. If needed, she can run a meeting and get the contract signed, or she can get people to say things they wouldn't have imagined saying to a lawyer and be thankful as a result. The power is in having the choice. She is the same authentic leader no matter what style she uses.

For so many of us, purpose says, "Really? You're planning to stay in that boring place? The curious little kid inside of you wants to play—let's go make it happen." I have seen that twinkle in many leaders' eyes when they have the choice of staying in style or listening to their purpose. Let's be clear that many people have chosen, even when they discover their purpose, to stay with one style. This isn't a magic pill. Yet in all my years, I haven't seen anything else that is as effective at kicking one into heaven, yelling and screaming all the way.

Experiencing our authenticity as a leader

There is a second important element connecting purpose to our authenticity as a leader. In all our programs, we ask the participants to list the qualities they need to see from themselves and their leaders for them to be authentic leaders. Here are the characteristics that show up again and again, in every kind of organization and context:

- Clarity of purpose
- Self-awareness, knowing your strengths and your weaknesses
- Openness to feedback both positive and negative
- Transparency with direct reports
- Living your values, especially when things are not going well
- Setting others up for success and helping them find their voice
- Delivering sustainable business results
- Ability to shift leadership styles to be appropriate yet be the same person
- Vision and able to energize the troops
- Empathy when it would be easy to be judgmental
- Efficiency at decision making
- Ability to show vulnerability as well as strength and know when each makes sense

The leadership traits vary only slightly from group to group, but here's the big catch:

- When did any of us actually work for someone who demonstrated all of these characteristics?

- Even more difficult to face, when did any of us actually demonstrate all of these characteristics ourselves?

Participants never lack passion to define what the perfect leader would look like. If I would let them, they would add to the list all day. Yet the gap between our desires or expectations and the imperfect beings that we all are is humbling.

This much I know: When each person steps fully into the room of purpose, when they are operating from that unique gift that they are, and we are in the presence of it, the fullest version of the list of characteristics shows up. It is as if someone switched on the lights. How they interact with the rest of their team and the level of leadership they bring to the situation is stunning. Does my embodiment of the characteristics look anything like yours? Probably not at all. Each of us has our own unique way to bring our leadership to the table. Some of us are low-key, others more extroverted; some more poetic, others direct.

And then, it all disappears....

One of the most challenging things about purpose is that we never operate from it 100 percent or all the time. We step into the room and with it comes a powerful set of leadership characteristics that we all value, and then 10 minutes later we step out. The challenge is to find a way to more easily get back into the room. We step out and we step in.

This is probably the most important connection between purpose and authentic leadership. To be genuinely authentic, we must own that sometimes we are leading from our purpose and sometimes we are not. Each of us is a work in progress. When we know our purpose, at some level we have a choice. We must each then choose.

Points to ponder

Review the list of compelling leadership characteristics:

- Clarity of purpose
- Self-awareness, knowing your strengths and your weaknesses
- Openness to feedback both positive and negative
- Transparency with direct reports
- Living your values, especially when things are not going well
- Setting others up for success and helping them find their voice
- Delivering sustainable business results
- Ability to shift leadership styles to be appropriate yet be the same person
- Vision and able to energize the troops
- Empathy when it would be easy to be judgmental
- Efficiency at decision making
- Ability to show vulnerability as well as strength and know when each makes sense

1. When did you work for someone who demonstrated many of these characteristics?
2. When have you demonstrated many of these characteristics?
3. When did you have the greatest growth and development in your life? Was it when your style was your answer to every question, or was it when you were put

in situations that demanded you stretch and integrate multiple styles?

4. How does purpose move you toward a deeper authenticity?
5. What is your preferred leadership style?
6. What does it mean to be the author of your leadership and life?

Chapter 9

IMPACT: STANDING ON SOLID GROUND

> We are all fragile when we don't know what our purpose
> is, when we haven't thrown ourselves with abandon into
> a social role, when we haven't committed ourselves to
> certain people, when we feel like a swimmer in an ocean
> with no edge.
>
> —David Brooks

Up until the twentieth century, most people were born into a family and vocation that defined their identity: You were a farmer, merchant, blacksmith, fisherman, or banker, and so were your parents and theirs before them. Your options were limited by circumstances you could not control. This was the case for everyone. Henry VIII was the King of England not because of his superior abilities to govern, but because his brother died and left him with the crown.

Our options are broader today. Many of us live in a world in which children and students are asked, "So, what do you want to be?" Right now, one of my daughters is spending a year at London's Globe Theater while in college studying to be an actress. The other is entering college with the desire to be a high school English teacher. We are not limited by external circumstances as in most of history, and yet we still set limits on how we define "who we are." Today, most of our identity (how we see ourselves and how we want others to see us) is based on our company, role, job, and status in life. When we go to a different country, the customs forms don't ask "Who are you?" They ask our occupation and how many dependents we have in tow. Unfortunately, for most of us that basic information sums up our identity. The significant ups and downs in our lives can be associated with what university we attended, the role we ascended to, and which organizations we have worked for.

What is our real identity?

In working with executives to define how they are going to lead from their purpose, we start by looking out five years to provide a wider vista of how purpose will manifest for each person. It's funny how, no matter what level they find themselves at now, many think that in five years the fullest expression of their purpose will be to be CEO, chairman of a company, head of HR or legal, or whatever the top of their current pyramid looks like. After all, most people believe that a CEO is a "better" identity than a managing director, and so on from there. Ironically, despite all this striving for the top, when I coach the senior leadership, what they really want is the job they had two levels *back*. Everyone seems to want the role they no longer have anymore, or should have stayed in if they knew then what they know now.

It's remarkable how much we allow our roles to change us. Executives will subject themselves to remarkable levels of inauthentic and purposeless activities in hopes of getting the coveted role, a further indictment of that way of looking at the value of our identity. I have lost count of the number of times I have seen and heard others comment that someone "changed" when they landed the big job. People say, "The minute he was promoted to the SVP role, he changed from being transparent, authentic, and real to controlling, protective, and confrontational." These roles do that because our sense of identity isn't strong enough to define how we should lead. We feel we must become a type of leader that "is a CEO," and this is not nearly as effective as the purpose that has been leading us all our life.

A desired role or position is a goal. It's great to have big goals, like being at the top of your field, winning a Nobel Prize, or joining the ranks of *Fortune*'s top 100 CEOs. These goals, if achieved, can be a wonderful stage to lead from your purpose. Once attained, the title or role in itself isn't who you are or the ultimate version of your purpose. How you do whatever role, job, or vocation you have is the gift of your purpose. Every CEO is unique, and so are you. The challenge becomes, does the role define you or do you define the role?

Letting our role define our identity is dangerous because all those roles and goals we chase after are fragile. In many cases, we can be replaced at any moment by another person "they" find more to their liking. Each externally defined role is dependent on someone else and what they decide for us. We give so much power to others in the organization to affect how we see ourselves. The more we see our identity validated or defined by these roles we desire, the more power we give to others to determine our fate. It's like being on a TV game show in which we compete with the other contestants for our identity. Are we a winner or a loser? I have seen executives become consumed by the desire for a title or role as if that determined their true worth in the world.

Another challenge is that even if we reach those lofty places, we can't stay in them forever. I spend a good deal of my time talking with ex-CEOs and department heads and formerly famous individuals, helping them find a deeper purpose that has always been there. These discussions are powerful and painful because their identities are based on something that is no more and never will be again. We all know people who repeatedly talk about who they used to be to everyone they meet. Luckily, this might be the perfect moment to access purpose, the one identity that will always be there as all others defined by the world are swept away.

On a layover in Dallas, I was having a glass of wine at one of those nondescript airport bars when a very professionally dressed executive sat down beside me and we started talking. He was a senior partner in one of the top four consulting firms and he had decided to retire early. We both had a long layover, so I offered to buy him another glass of wine if he would share his reasoning with me. He described his career, from an undergraduate degree at the University of Michigan to his first job, getting into Harvard Business School, being recruited by the consulting firm he now represented, and his crazed desire to be the youngest consultant to make it to each of the next levels in the organization. We both laughed ruefully as he described how every time he was about to be the youngest one to get to the next level, someone else would get there first. In the end, he wasn't the youngest, but he was an exceptional senior partner. At that moment in the airport bar, his role and title no longer mattered. Showing me the sailboat he had just bought, which in a month would be his new residence, he summed up his decision process. "You know, I spent all my life letting other people determine who I should be, if I was good enough, when I would be allowed into the next inner circle. When I arrived at the top, I realized all I got to deal with was all the people below me who wanted in. I realized I never really felt at home doing all the things I had to do to get where I am now. It's a rat race for someone else to be fooled by. I have decided to close this chapter out and finally just be myself."

We spent the rest of our time together talking about his new life and the things he now could do, say, and be, that had been stifled for years.

There is another major trip wire that can cause great mischief relative to our identity and the impact we have on others. For many of us, our identity is more connected with our profession or area of expertise, rather than a title or role. "I am a doctor, lawyer, consultant, engineer..." has been with us much longer than any title or role we held for just a couple of years.

Over time, I have read thousands of leadership 360-degree review reports prior to working with groups of executives. A consultant interviews 6 to 10 people who work with the executive (his or her boss, employees, peers, and others) and creates a four- to six-page report summarizing the world's view of the exec's strengths, weaknesses, and areas for development. The first half of the report focuses on how each of these people is the best in what they do. It's why they have their current job. The second half is a detailed assessment of what each of these people must work on—yes, their warts—and all are defined in detail. These are the issues that, if not addressed, will dramatically limit any future possibilities.

When I read the warts-and-all sections, I usually see things like this:

Jim needs to be even more ready to delegate, rather than carrying too much of the load himself, as is his tendency given his domain expertise, drive, energy, and personal capacity.

Steve's attention to detail and drive for rigor can lead him too often to fall back on his own expertise, rather than delegating more confidently and relying on the resources of his team.

Samanthas energy, drive, and mastery of the topic mean that she tends to dive straight into solution mode in her urge to get things done, without necessarily allowing her team the opportunity to work things through for themselves. She needs to learn to hold back from the detail, to delegate and empower more readily, and to focus her personal energies on delivery through others.

When discussing these comments with the Jims, Steves, and Samanthas of the world, we eventually get around to the underlying issue. For many it comes down to the fact that they are just so much better at what they do than the people who work for them. If they don't do it, it probably won't get done at the level of quality that is needed. This robs everyone in the situation, as the people who should be doing the work don't learn and the leaders, who I am working with, aren't doing what they should be doing.

What many of these leaders realize as we dig deeper is that they pause at hiring someone who is as good as they are at the task. At some level, they don't want to give up being the senior expert. It's who they see themselves as being. If they really hire someone as good or, God forbid, better than them, who are they? We could say it's good news they haven't adopted an identity based on their new leadership role—many of them admit that the new role feels foreign to them—yet they like the influence, pay, and status that go with it. We all know people who like the goodies of the role but are still doing the job of the next level below them. It's the ultimate trap of seeing their identity as their area of expertise.

Of course, moving into a new role or position takes time and there is always lots to learn. It's a challenge regardless of how we define ourselves, but it is much more difficult if our identity is wrapped up in our expertise.

Reclaiming solid ground

Purpose is the wonderful antidote to basing your identity on your profession, expertise, role, job, or organization. Purpose has always been there and always will be there. Your purpose doesn't change and nobody can take it away from you. The more you invest in it, listen to it, and operate from it, the stronger it becomes. Few things in life are like this, and it's one of the reasons that having clarity about your purpose is so powerful.

When we face challenging times, we need something solid to stand on, especially when everything around us feels unstable. Purpose provides that needed stability. It creates resilience because when we operate from purpose our identity is no longer at the mercy of everything outside us. Think about how you answer the question "Who are you?" What goes into your definition of your identity? What happens if your identity is not defined by the external world? Purpose gives us the right to own our unique gift and bring it to every situation in life, from the inside out versus the outside in. We are no longer the future, current, or former X, Y, or Z. We are that which we have always been and will always be, our purpose. That is something you can depend on and lead from in the worst of times as well as the best of times.

Ranjay, whom we met in chapter 3, tells a great story that reinforces the power of a purpose-driven identity. Ranjay's purpose statement is "Bring people to center stage. Lights, camera, action, we make a difference." Some time ago, Ranjay was up for a big promotion and he felt certain that he would get the job. Yet, someone else was given the job.

> When I feel low and lousy, when bad things happen, I remember the concept of *equifinality*: there are many ways to get to where you need to be. I felt let down. I wondered, "Is this based on performance or chemistry, or what?" Everyone was trying to say nice things

to me: "You will get the next one," and so on. I spent a few days in reflection mode, and I realized my purpose was the one thing nobody could take away from me—it was my leading light. I sat back and said, "In life there are many different roles I play, and in some there will be disappointments—as in this instance—but at the same time there are many other (arguably more) aspects of my life that are going well (at home, for example), which give me a lot of joy. It's time to acknowledge that!" My purpose is always there to pull me toward my sources of positive energy, rather than allowing the negative aspects to pull me down. I realized happiness lies in bringing many other things to center stage and letting go of all the pain associated with not getting a bigger job or with a delayed promotion. My purpose was my inner voice!

There were some people on my team who were waiting for a promotion or big career move and who were perhaps in worse shape than me. "I need to get them taken care of" was the message from my purpose. "If I falter now, maybe these people will be affected. We have a major HR plan to finish and a big milestone to achieve— opening a new training center, which was a massive project my team had worked on for the last two years. My team needed me; my work needed me. I put all my energy into this. I did everything in my power to do a great job. We had a world-class launch of the training center, cutting through all the politics and doing our jobs. The best thing happened: my people got the promotions and big moves they so richly deserved. I was so happy! The work showed, and the rest is history. Instead of focusing on the disappointment, focus on what you can do. Looking into and leading from my purpose gives me joy or at least courage in the face of hardship. And then equifinality indeed prevailed: I got a huge promotion to run a large region, which was never my plan, but which truly allowed me to lead from my purpose by a factor of 10.

We all have faced a situation like Ranjay's. It's almost impossible not to over the course of a career. The real power of purpose is to be the solid ground we stand on and to define how we respond to the situation. Ranjay could easily have lost his motivation, become distracted, and left his team without an advocate. Instead he let the identity that was fragile fall away and in doing so deepened his relationship with his purpose.

By letting our roles define us, most of us set ourselves up for situations like the one Ranjay experienced. The good news is, he has his purpose to help him. Many times, I have had the opportunity to watch the shift happen in real time while I am working with an executive. You see the grip of the desire for a role and then, as they step into their purpose, they begin to see a different and more satisfying path. We have many roles, and before we know our purpose, who we are is represented by the small space in the center that is common across these roles. Yet our identity tends to be strongly defined by one of the three. Each is fragile in its own way; losing one of them can have a significantly destabilizing impact.

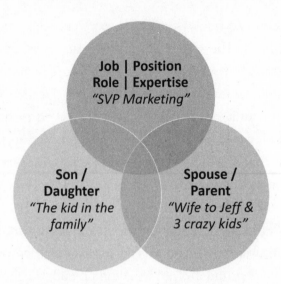

After we align ourselves with the purpose that is leading us, we have a different relationship with the various roles we play.

JAMES—To harness *all* the elements to win the race.

For example, when I met James, he was a senior procurement executive in a large multinational. His purpose is "To harness *all* the elements to win the race." We discovered his purpose statement through his lifelong passion for sailing. He grew up sailing and was so good at it that he was selected as an Olympic team alternate. Sailing a three-man skiff requires unbelievable balance and coordination. "You never know what the wind will do next, and, in the end, it's only your combined capabilities, intuition, and flow that win the race. All our competitors have the same boats we have…so it's all about the crew and how you read the elements."

This made great sense for his career in procurement, and it was satisfying to watch him shift from defining his identity as a procurement guy or as a sailor—both strong roles—to realizing that, in everything he did, James was his purpose. When you lead a global procurement job the smallest little things add up to big savings, and the same is true for racing a sailboat.

Yet when we first looked at his ideas for how he was going to more fully lead from his purpose over the next five years, James saw only one role. The only words he had to "define" the fullest expression of his purpose five years in the future were "head of procurement for a global multinational."

I wanted him to see that the role of head of procurement doesn't define how he would fulfill leading from his purpose. It's okay to have a goal, but that goal by itself is in no way an expression of anything other than hard work, luck, tenacity, and having the right person want you. I asked, "If we look through the lens of your purpose, no matter what job you end up in, what will people say about the way you lead?" James realized that the answers were the same regardless of his future position.

I am known for training the best crews and winning big races. The unique qualities of my leadership are...

- I can be masterful in an unpredictable global world.
- I see the wind shears before others and get the crew positioned to get that little extra speed.
- Everyone feels that they are in the same boat to win the same race no matter which business they are supporting.
- I am the one who is calm when we don't win the race; we learn from the loss and set up for the next race.

As you can see, James began to understand that his purpose offered him a very different way to look at his identity and his impact. The lens through which he sees the world applies to every part of his life. Notice that we now understand the unique way he will lead as opposed to what title he holds.

James added a final facet of leading from his purpose "To harness *all* the elements to win the race": his family.

Reinvest in my shore team (my family)

- We as a family have our "thing" we do that binds us.

One of the biggest "unlocks" of purpose is that it allows us to bring all the parts of our life into focus. We don't just live our purpose at work. Given James's commitment and focus on his procurement career, things at home had been neglected. Home is as important a place to live his purpose as his job. Bringing his purpose to his family had immediate impact. Many executives are already leading from their purpose at work when we meet them. They may not know the words that best define their purpose, yet they are fully leading from it anyway. But their purpose often remains unexpressed at home. If our identity is based on our job, then it shouldn't surprise anyone that we spend all our time and energy on that while neglecting the other roles in our life. When our identity is based on our purpose, we can live it in all parts of our life.

Recently I had the opportunity to interview James. I had not talked with him in four years and was curious to know how things had turned out. The good news is, he is clear that his sense of identity is based on his purpose. Ironically, the global procurement role he was so attached to when we last spoke is now history. He left the multinational to become head of procurement for a very small airline. Why? Well, he now lives 100 meters from a world-class sailing club where his kids are learning how to race. This allows him to fulfill his purpose with his family. As his boys grew up, he realized there was one window of time—the present—when he could really bring his purpose to them and his wife. James traded off his desire for a global procurement role for what would best allow him to lead from his purpose in all parts of his life. He stopped letting his job define him and instead defined himself through his purpose.

What happens when we not only see our own identity based on purpose but also begin to interact with others through the purpose that leads them? For most of us, this has probably taken place when others have helped us see what we ourselves could not see without help.

Engaging others through purpose instead of roles

I have had the privilege of helping many executives make the shift from a role to a purpose-based identity, yet I had missed seeing one of the most powerful impacts of this transformation—one that I would never have figured out if not for many late-evening discussions with alumni across many programs. Alums come to the program to share their stories about the impact of purpose, yet the evening discussions often turn to stories about conversations that have had a big impact on them. There is a pattern—most alumni feel that two or three conversations were deeply powerful over the course of their lives, while others were not.

Think about the thousands of serious conversations people have had with you. Many people have spoken to you in earnest about something you should or shouldn't do—and, let's face it, most of the time their words don't really take hold. If you think about it, only a couple of conversations had a profound impact. They changed what you did and in many cases how you saw yourself. In recent years, we have asked over 500 alumni of our programs about this phenomenon. We have found three common themes.

- **The effective conversations were tough ones.** Rarely were these pleasant chats acknowledging or praising us for something we'd done well. On the contrary, the conversation was almost always one in which we were pulled aside and given a tough message.
- **The other person was an authority or a family member.** The person speaking either had a level of authority that made

us believe what they said was "true," or it was a loved family member. Many times, it was a senior leader who sat us down in our youth for a tough and direct discussion about how we were showing up and what was going to be needed instead.

- **The person spoke to our bigger sense of who we are**: our purpose.

We have all had dozens of tough talks from senior leaders and family members, but their impact and long-term results are mixed. What makes the difference and causes change is *who* they were speaking to. They weren't speaking to the person who had screwed up or was screwing up. They spoke to the deeper purpose inside us. They didn't use those words, but they knew, and we knew that they knew. This is so rare that it has a memorable impact when it happens. What's more, it can't be faked. If they were just there to congratulate us on how great we were, limited authenticity would be required. If they were calling us up short and at the same time calling us to who we really are, that's a beautiful and rare thing. When it happens, we don't forget it.

Calling someone into their purpose has the most positive impact when it would be easy to see the other person as a problem, failing to deliver on their role, needing a whack on the side of the head so to speak. We all know how that feels.

In a previous life, I designed and managed large corporate change efforts. I was trained by the best and was the person whose experience brought calm and security to the client and the other consultants. I was appointed the role of architecture lead for a worldwide rollout that would affect tens of thousands of employees. The complexity wasn't an issue, but the chemistry was. The two senior people, one French and the other a lifelong Houston oilman, were totally different, making the dynamics challenging. I didn't like either of them, they didn't like me, and they didn't like or trust each other. I was very much stuck in my identity as an expert on large-scale change. I was right, and they were wrong, and it was my job to "help" them not do stupid things. You can imagine how this came across.

Thomas, my boss, who was 25 years my senior, sat me down. He started the discussion with, "How's it going?" I described all that was happening and what should be done to fix the problem "out there." Thomas looked right at me. "Nick, I really know who you are. You are bright, quick, solving unsolvable problems, and dedicated, so help me understand how this is working for you." Truth be told, it wasn't working, and it was never going to work; the chemistry was just not there. In the end, we moved the lead role to a colleague who was a perfect match for our French/Houston combo and he stayed in that role for many years.

As I look back at that moment, Thomas saw the deeper truth of who I was, which, based on what I know now, is aligned 100 percent with my purpose. He cracked open the door to the room of purpose that I know as the unique gift that I bring to the world. I just didn't have words for it then. Instead of feeling like I had been reassigned or fired, I felt seen and validated. Instead of being destroyed, my identity was strengthened.

Once again, how we define our identity and those of others dramatically changes what is achieved. Remember the improvement in job satisfaction and engagement that purpose can bring. Think of the place you lead from and how you see others as the lens that purpose lets you look through: with it, we see a very different impact on others.

My belief is the person who spoke to us in this way was operating from his or her purpose in that conversation. This is what a purposeful dialogue looks and feels like.

The impact of purpose is that it not only gives us an identity that is finally ours, it also allows us to honor others in a way they too can operate more from their purpose. Each of us needs to be reminded of where we find solid ground.

Points to ponder

1. Who are you—what makes up your identity today?
2. In your current position, how much of your identity is defined by your title or role or by the work you do (just a little, some, or a big part)?
3. Do you define your role, or does your role define you?
4. Which of your professional roles has had the most impact on your identity? Why?
5. What have been the two or three most powerful discussions others have had with you in your life?
6. What is the common pattern across those experiences?
7. What elements of purpose do you believe may be there for you to find from these discussions?
8. When did you last speak to someone's deeper purpose (as opposed to their role, title, or personality)?
9. What was the impact on him or her?

Chapter 10

IMPACT: THE TRUE SOURCE OF ENERGY

Purpose gives me energy. It's what gets you up in the morning and drives you. It gives you direction.... You're one part of the journey of something bigger. It keeps going. Purpose is always expanding.

—John

I have a very strong feeling when I am in or not in my purpose.... When in my purpose, I have an abundance of energy. I feel I am on fire. I notice now when I'm not in my purpose the heaviness comes.

—Stacey

Few things are more important or desirable to leaders than high levels of energy and engagement. When we have it, all goes well. When we don't, life sucks. I've been struck by how many leaders tell me about the energy and renewed engagement they get from their purpose. Increased energy and engagement are things you can't fake: When we have energy, we can deal with anything; when we're drained, leading gets hard and leading authentically gets harder. We drink Red Bull and Starbucks, get exercise and a good night's sleep, but in my world and yours it's just not enough. You either have energy that permeates your being, or you just don't have what it takes, and you feel disengaged. We all know what it feels like to give a presentation with all the energy we can muster, knowing that the tank is empty. We believe (or hope) nobody notices, but at some level they know. It's hard to come up with the right stuff—energy, engagement, and authenticity— when we are not operating from purpose.

So much of leading is about how you motivate, energize, and empower others. Yet so much that is done in support of these objectives is deeply unsatisfying in the end.

What disengagement looks like

It's not only senior leaders who have a problem finding energy and engagement. Organizations struggle to promote employee engagement, a metric that human resource professionals consider to be a critical driver of business success. According to Investopedia, "Engaged employees care about their work and about the performance of the company, and feel that their efforts make a difference." Gallup has published research on engagement levels in organizations across 145 countries. Their latest numbers are not encouraging (see graphic page 148).

I don't know about you, but when I look at these numbers I am just stunned. The fact that 87 percent of people at work are asleep or running away is just crazy-making. Let's assume that in most organizations it's only half as bad as the numbers suggest.

Gallup–Company Engagement for 145 Countries

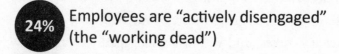 Employees are "actively disengaged"
(the "working dead")

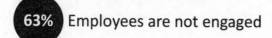 Employees are not engaged

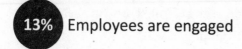 Employees are engaged

Even if the number of "disengaged" and "not engaged" is, let's say, only 43.5 percent, it's too many. In fact, I've seen many "not engaged" or "disengaged" people—they show up in front of me almost every week. They look like you and they are sitting in our programs. The reality is, the energy and engagement that we feel is not at the level we wish it to be. "Fake it till you make it" may work at times and in some cases, but over the long haul we just feel exhausted.

Many of the executives I have worked with have "arrived"— they are at the place that everyone else is desperate to get to. What you find when you arrive is a set of issues and human dilemmas that suck all your energy and make you wish you could become one of the actively disengaged.

- You must decide who will get a key role when both internal candidates are great, they are your former peers, and one is a good friend. The decision you make will send all kinds of messages. And there is only one position—so, no matter what, you lose.

- You are told to make deep cost cuts while maintaining top-level growth and, by the way, don't impact the long term. No magic elves are available to solve this puzzle.
- You spend all your time fighting battles with corporate for your people and no longer actually "do" anything fun.
- When you look at the people above you, you see that their lives are a complete disaster.
- You are the one everyone talks about at the bar and when you show up they act like someone died.
- There aren't enough hours in the day or days in the week to accomplish your workload, but everything you don't do lands back in your lap and needs twice as much effort to fix. Those emails you didn't read are boring holes in your soul while you sleep....
- The senior leadership "team" can't agree among themselves, which means your long-term strategy plan never gets approved. But those same people still hold you responsible for the results.
- When key resources you depend on leave, there really isn't anyone but you to plug the gap for the next six months—so now you have twice as much to do.

Remember, this "and much, much more" is the reward you get if you arrive at one of the top roles in an organization! My point is that there really isn't any place to "get to." Rather, there is a place to lead from. Purpose genuinely transforms that list from a vise that's about to crush your little head into a compelling adventure.

Finding engagement, fulfillment, and energy

Research by Aon Hewitt suggests that employee engagement has for many years been the cornerstone of a company's success in both doing well and doing good. Employees with a strong sense of purpose are more satisfied, engaged, and fulfilled, becoming higher performers who are more productive and committed to the organization. But recently there has been a decline in employee engagement, pointing to a concerning trend in human capital.

Luckily, there seems to be an antidote to this downward trend. Pioneering firms are attempting to shift toward enabling employees to be purpose-driven advocates for their mission, and to transition the thinking from "employee engagement" to "employee fulfillment." Through shifting the focus, companies are using purpose to inspire and engage employees.

We have already cited evidence of the importance of purpose to millennials, but it is not just millennials and gen Xers who are following this trend. Baby boomers are leading the generational charge on shifting toward purpose-oriented fulfillment.

A joint study by LinkedIn and Imperative highlights that purpose-oriented workers are 64 percent more likely to find fulfillment in their jobs and 73 percent more likely to find job satisfaction. This indicates that companies with a clearly articulated and well-branded organizational purpose can attract better talent through their recruitment process and benefit from low employee turnover.

Why is it that purpose seems to have such a direct impact on energy and engagement? How can purpose help us address the crazy stuff we all face in our work world?

From what I have witnessed, purpose and energy spring from the same place. That's probably why they are so closely connected. After all, what is your unique gift, other than an access point of energy for you and those you touch? Every time I meet a person whose purpose is clear, our conversation leaves both of us feeling more energized no matter how serious or "heavy" the topic. It is like putting on a set of special glasses, looking at the same crazy situation, and seeing a different set of options.

One of our biggest challenges in our day-to-day journeys as leaders is finding the energy to keep moving. When the leaders I work with surrender to their purpose, they tell me that their energy level goes up by a factor of five. Purpose is the core essence of who you are—by its very nature, it is the fuel that creates the energy that is yours. High-value energy and engagement are common themes with all the leaders we have interviewed.

Remember, discovering one's purpose is not an intellectual exercise for the leaders I've worked with. There's almost a predictable energy pattern around the discovery process. When they access their purpose it's as if someone turned the lights up bright in the room and the theme music to their favorite movie started playing very loudly. Everyone else in the room feels it, knows it, and is energized as well when purpose shows up. Amazingly, the answer to the question "What is my purpose?" comes from the crazy adventures of our life that look no different from the confusing and complex issues we are in the middle of right now as we lead in our current context. From there we find a level of energy and engagement that turns our response from "run away and hide" into "lean in" and brings the curious child inside us to the moment.

Didier Dallemagne is an interesting example of this. Didier

discovered his purpose at the end of his corporate career, three years before retirement.

> We were in the corporate training center, where I have been numerous times, usually quite depressed as we were reminded of what we didn't do well. This time, when I called my wife, she said, "Are you sure you are at the training center? Because you sound so energetic, so positive—it is not your usual mood when you are there." I think that finding your purpose is enormously energizing. When I linked my own purpose with the purpose of the business, I could really translate that to mission and purpose for my brands. That is extraordinary because you can create energy in your organization and coalesce people behind a purpose. It is not one or the other. When you have something in line with your business it is fantastic. Purpose gives energy; it is an opportunity to lead a group of people with that energy.

Another touch point that helped me realize the connection between purpose and energy is when someone is stuck and can't articulate the purpose that is leading them. Sometimes when I run a three-day program and a couple of participants just cannot uncover the deeper purpose that has been leading them all their life, there is a low energy level—almost desperation. They are frustrated and agitated and go home to a few sleepless nights. Almost invariably, I get a call a few weeks later and one of two things happens:

1. They tell me their clarified purpose statement; the level of energy and impact on those around them is dramatic and

clear. It's like they have become plugged into a universal wall socket of energy.

2. We do the final piece of work right there on the phone. Things shift in real time and—*boom!*—the energy uptake is immediate. We both experience it. It's not as if we need to check a five-point list of criteria to determine that we have hit the place of purpose and energy. We both feel it.

We have all been energized in our life. The reason we desire it is because we know how great it feels and recognize its impact on others. Our purpose gives us easy access to that place where the energy resides. Need to give a big presentation, even though you didn't sleep much the night before? Remember your purpose. Have to keep yourself going with a grueling schedule of multiple site visits in which the people at the last site deserve the same amount of you as those at the first? Step into your purpose. Have to deal with client or a boss cutting you apart in a meeting and leaving your last six months of work on the floor? Ask your purpose how you should look at what just happened. You want energy? Talk to your purpose (literally).

NIC BRASSEY—To release the Madiba (Mandela) magic, with a balance of enthusiasm and humility.

One leader who exemplifies this is Nic Brassey. Instead of sharing just one element of Nic's journey, I think it will be helpful to see his whole journey and how purpose, energy, engagement, chaos, paradox, and moral dilemmas can all coexist.

Nic Brassey was raised in South Africa, where he witnessed

the apartheid system firsthand. He went to a mixed-race school and saw what his friends across the racial divide had to go through. All people of color had to live in segregated communities known as townships. Nic could go home and do his homework while his friends had to deal with verbal and physical violence in their everyday lives. Sometimes his friends would go home to the township and return days later, badly beaten and telling stories that horrified Nic. Was Nic harmed? No, his challenge was to live in a system that sucked the life energy out of everyone. Many of his friends were either oppressed or trained to be the oppressors in a system that was morally corrupt.

Apartheid ended about the time Nic graduated from college and was choosing a career. Fortunately, forced army conscription had ended. Most of his white friends decided to follow the money and go off to banking. He decided to go in the opposite direction and work at an adult education center. For two years, he taught 55- to 60-year-old black men to read and write. The men tested him every day—they couldn't understand why he was doing this. They told him their life stories of being treated as third-class citizens and he listened. He saw these men cry tears of joy because they could now read to their grandchildren, help them do their homework, take a bus, or read a newspaper and no longer feel the shame of illiteracy. If you want a reason to get out of bed every morning, there couldn't be a better one. Nic felt so absolutely energized by what he was doing that it became the foundation for how he saw himself and decided what mattered. If it didn't create this level of energy in him, it wasn't worth doing. Instead of running away from the fallout from apartheid, Nic was thriving in how he faced it. Nic knew there are different kinds of leadership—open ones that help people grow as opposed to more closed or traditional ones—and he was clear about which kind he was going to be an expression of.

Many years later he was brought in to close a factory of 300 employees in Atlanta, Georgia. He had a choice of how to do the closure. He could close the factory quickly and move on, which would be easiest for him, or he could keep the factory open much longer. The second option would force him to deal with the morale issues and address the choices people faced after they lost their jobs. Once again, energy was the key for him. There was no "energy" in just closing the plant. What energized Nic was how proud the people were of their work, and he wanted them to leave that way. Working with the Georgia Department of Labor, he managed to redeploy all but one person. He kept the factory open to the end, so people had the pride of closing the place right. Instead of being an energy drain, the small things he did to help every person gave him energy and positive memories. He received an award for the outcome. It is possible to do difficult things and still see people flourish and help them move on to new and potentially more interesting places. Here is Nic Brassey's purpose statement: "To release the Madiba (Mandela) magic, with a balance of enthusiasm and humility."

Recently, Nic had the challenge we mentioned earlier: pulling off a big presentation and accessing that deeper well of purpose. Nic had been dreading having to run a one-day inspirational session for his firm's top 400, *in Dutch*. He had only recently moved to Holland to take a senior VP HR role and had dug into learning the language. It would be intimidating for anyone to run a session in a language they were just learning; to do it for the top

400 would give many of us a panic attack. He wanted to give back to the audience something special about the company. In Nic's words, "I dispelled any fear or anxious thoughts and felt a great spike of energy." You could say that Nic sounded arrogant; after all, what could he know about the company after being there for such a short time? Yet, from the room of purpose, just as he had in South Africa and Atlanta, he knew there was a way to do something that was high energy and full of impact. He decided to focus the session on the theme of liberating talent in the organization through storytelling. He realized the key would be to allow the best stories to be brought up on stage for everyone to experience. Nic's unique gift was to lead the session in a way that helped people who had never told their stories find themselves on stage, highlighting their talents to the whole organization as role models of the change to be created. For most of us, our experience of telling our stories about our talents starts and ends with job interviews. From then on, the only things we hear about are what we aren't doing and our weaknesses. Nic turned this upside down. His intervention was energizing and engaging at its core and completely an expression of his purpose. People still talk to him about it.

Of course, Nic isn't perfect; none of us are. Our purpose compels us to step more fully into leading from our purpose, especially when doing so isn't comfortable. Being energized and engaged when things are going well or, we are amazing, is easy. You don't need purpose to show up then. Nic's challenge in his role now is to not be the person who solves everyone's problems. He is in that part of his career where being the subject expert that got him to his current position is what will get in the way.

As we have learned, when we shift our sense of identity from our expertise to our purpose, we find solid ground to lead from. Nic's orientation needs to shift from expert to general manager and coach. He is very aware of how much his expertise has been getting in the way. "I understand why I do that, but it gets in the way of my purpose." Remember Nic's purpose is "To release the Madiba (Mandela) magic, with a balance of enthusiasm and humility."

He has realized that, as he gets more senior, leadership behavior that fixes things for others doesn't help him live his purpose; on the contrary, it keeps him bogged down in the weeds of the organization. Fixing things or doing something that might be rote or easy for him doesn't help others to be as successful as they can. It is well intended, but its outcome is the opposite of making people succeed and, even though it is "easy" for him, it uses energy instead of generating it. Nic is working on this, and he has a great metaphor that those of us who enjoy wine will appreciate: "Like a good bottle of wine, I need to let my leadership skills age." Nic realizes that his leadership behavior hasn't caught up to his purpose. He recognizes that this moment is a life-changing opportunity because it is a transition from the world he has been living in to senior leadership maturity, which is the world he wants to live in for the coming years. "I feel the need to be more hands-on. It creates tension when I want to marshal resources to help others be successful, instead of helping them marshal their resources to reach their targets."

Nic has these "conversations" with his purpose all the time. This is the power of purpose. How do we engage and become energized by our own insights about who we are and who we are becoming? Purpose is the only force I know of that honors where we have come from and, at the same time, calls us to step into a bigger set of shoes in our life. Nic is in a huge transition from how he has seen himself to a new role he is ready to step into. What allows that to happen is that his identity is now grounded in his purpose as opposed to his role or skills. His source of energy is something that can't be taken away from him, even though acting in a new way can be stressful at times. In the next chapter we will learn some surprising things about stress and how to manage it.

Points to ponder

1. How does the organization you work for compare to the Gallup scores on engagement?
2. In terms of energy levels, on a scale of 1 to 10 (where 1 is the lowest and 10 the highest), how do you score in your current role?
3. What activities bring you the most energy?
4. What activities drain your energy?
5. What percentage of your time do you feel energized as opposed to not energized?
6. What would happen if you got a 30 percent increase in energy level?

IMPACT: STRESS THAT'S GOOD FOR YOU

> Can you imagine a climber scaling the wall of ice
> at Everest's Lhotse Face and saying, "This is such a
> hassle"? . . . The climber knows the context of his stress.
> It has personal meaning to him; he has chosen it.
>
> —Kelly McGonigal

We all have stress in our life. Do you see yours as your version of climbing Mount Everest, or do you see it as a problem that should go away? If there is anything that purpose impacts, it's our relationship to stress. Yes, *stress*, that thing that everyone says is bad for us, turns out to be good for us when it's connected to our purpose. I am in debt to Kelly McGonigal of Stanford University for her insights on how stress can be good for us. Her insights have helped me understand a phenomenon I had noticed when I interviewed and observed executives. Many of them jump into very high-stress situations once they have their purpose clear. Like most people, I once believed that lots of stress was bad for you. Repeatedly, leaders have told me that they felt so much more stressed once they were leading from their purpose.

At the same time, they felt more alive, curious, and courageous. How could both be true?

It turns out that living your purpose tends to increase the level of stress in your life, significantly. Many of the stories highlighted in this book are about situations in which someone chooses a set of actions that dramatically increase his or her stress levels. Yes, that scary thing that everyone says is bad for you is a sign that you are leading from purpose. The good news is that purpose and the meaning it brings recalibrate our relationship to stress.

Adventures in purpose and stress

Stress is a serious topic, but I want to start this chapter with a funny story. I frequently facilitate three-day sessions for alumni of our Authentic Leadership and Purpose program. Recently I brought a group of four senior leaders together for one of these events and, on the Saturday afternoon, decided to take them sailing on the small boat I keep in a nearby lake.

Before you read the story, look at this group's purpose statements. You have already met most of these people in earlier chapters.

- **STACEY**—To ignite the worthy fight and blow your hair back
- **JOSTEIN**—To thrive in ambiguity and paradox for things that matter
- **CHRISTINA**—To help people who are flying kites to build a rocket

- **MIGUEL**—To be the captain of storytelling that lights people up to change the world
- **NICK**—To wake you up, and have you finally be home

Think about the types of situations you would expect a group of people with purpose statements like these to find themselves in. Would it be a stable and calm sailing adventure, or a wild storm in which all might be lost?

Bare Hill Pond Lake is one of those quintessential New England spots with a beach, kids playing in the water, and sailboats in the distance. I checked the weather and noted that later in the evening we would probably have a thunderstorm. "Okay," I said, "we'll get out a little early and everything will be fine." Two group members were seasoned sailors—what could go wrong? Besides, my sailboat is a trimaran; it has a main hull and two sealed outer pontoons, making it…almost…impossible to capsize.

With good wine, sushi, and other essentials, we headed out on the lake. We were sailing, everyone was having a great time, and the clouds began to gather. I checked the radar app and announced, "We should be fine if we begin to turn toward home." Christina asked Jostein, a world-class sailor, if the boat could capsize. He replied, "It's practically impossible to capsize these things." A minute later, a 50-mile-per-hour burst of wind hit us, and, in slow motion, the boat began to capsize!

Wine, sushi, cell phones, and most of the group were thrown into the water. Fortunately, the boat ended up only two-thirds capsized, for reasons I never really figured out. Christina, who had asked if the boat could turn over, was hanging upside down in the boat. "It's time to let go," we told her, "this boat isn't going anyplace."

Meanwhile, the storm was bearing down on us and the wind and waves were picking up. During it all, everyone was extremely calm and focused. What I didn't realize at the time was that each person in this group has a purpose that is about being calm in the storm. They weren't just calm, they were more alive and present than they had been the last two days. There was no drama, no hysterics, no yelling, just a calm set of voices figuring out what to do next. Stacey pointed to a powerboat and waved as she said, "This is so much more fun than sailing!"

The powerboat pulled up, "Do you need any help?" Two of our crew swam over and climbed aboard. The three of us who were supposed to be the experienced sailors were now at a loss: How do you turn a trimaran back over?

If it's impossible to capsize, it's damn hard to get back up.

Miguel realized that if we had one 50-mile-per-hour blast of wind, we just had to wait for the next one. He was thinking much more clearly than I was—I was still stuck on how the boat turned over in the first place. He and Jostein suggested that we use our weight to get the boat to an angle from which it would tip back over. Miguel and I pulled with all our strength as the world-class sailor pulled up the sail, which was deep in the water.

A boom of wind hit us; very slowly, we did the impossible and righted the boat. We were now in the middle of the lake in a sailboat half full of water, trying to sail to the nearest shore before the storm fully hit. The tornado warning horn started going off—we really didn't have much time.

We slowly sailed and bailed; we reached the other side and tied the boat to a tree, hoping it would be there after the storm.

The people on the powerboat picked us up and raced at top speed to the safety of the dock.

When we all piled in to the car, the group said in chorus, "Let's do it again!" When the howls of laughter stopped, I realized that what this group just did is what they are designed to do in life. Their jobs and purposes throw them into situations like this and they thrive in them.

We left the beach and returned to my home to find a tree down and power lines sparking on the driveway. Most people would freak out at this, but not this group. One of the crew calmly moved the power line aside. We found some more wine and hung out that night retelling the story of our adventures and waiting for the power to be restored.

I often see members of this group at gatherings of participants who are eager to hear what seasoned alumni have to say. They tell this damn story, which gets everyone laughing so hard and makes the point: The stories that you share over a bottle of wine—the ones that have the most drama, laughter, and magic—are often the ones most filled with stress, and purpose. Welcome to the show that purpose brings; may you cherish stress as you would a gifted friend.

How stress works

What is stress, then? Stress is created when there is a real or perceived threat to our well-being. The feeling of stress is our system's attempt to address the threat. There are several ways we can respond to stress; the one that we hear about most often is called the fight-or-flight response.

The "classic hits" of the fight-or-flight response include panicking just before we must give a presentation to a large group, going blank on an important exam, being shaken and tongue-tied when our boss's boss takes us apart in front of everyone, selling everything when the stock market goes down, or imagining the worst when we've run out of gas in the wrong part of town and someone approaches (who offers to help).

Real or imagined, a stressful event causes our body's sympathetic nervous system to react with the fight-or-flight response. The body produces more cortisol and adrenaline, triggering a higher heart rate, a significant increase in energy, heightened muscle preparedness, increased blood pressure, sweating, and alertness—all needed to help us protect ourselves if we are physically threatened. To do this our body makes tradeoffs, slowing down nonessential body functions, including our digestive and immune systems. That is why extended levels of this type of stress end up making us run-down and prone to illness.

The paradox of purpose

Purpose will have you step more readily into stressful situations. As Kelly McGonigal reminds us,

> If you put a wider lens on your life and subtract every day that you have experienced as stressful, you won't find yourself with an ideal life. Instead, you'll find yourself also subtracting the experiences that have helped you grow, the challenges you are most proud of, and

the relationships that define you. You may have spared yourself some discomfort, but you will also have robbed yourself of some meaning.

Imagine if you were asked to rate your response to this statement from 1 to 10: "Taking all things together, I feel my life is meaningful." Then you're asked to define the number of stressful events in your life. A team of researchers from Stanford and Florida State University did just that with a broad sample of U.S. adults ranging from 18 to 78 years of age. They found that those people who considered their lives to be most meaningful also reported not the least number of stressful events, but the most. In a similar vein, the ones under stress at the time of the study indicated that they found their lives more meaningful than the "lucky" individuals who were not under stress at the time.

This and other data led McGonigal to conclude, "Stress seems to be an inevitable consequence of engaging in roles and pursuing goals that feed our sense of purpose."

In a 10-year study of over 9,000 adults in the United Kingdom, those with highly stressful and meaningful lives had a 30 percent decrease in mortality at every age.

Let's add to the mystery. Gallup researchers polled more than 125,000 people from 121 countries, asking one question: Did you feel a great deal of stress yesterday? They then mapped the stress index scores to each country's index scores on well-being, life expectancy, and GDP. They expected to find that high stress indexes mapped to low positive index scores. Surprisingly, the opposite is true. Country by country, well-being, long life expectancy, and higher GDP coincide with higher stress indexes.

Higher levels of stress correlate to better health, higher living standards, and greater sense of community.

What happened to all the negative implications of stress?

What does good stress look like?

It turns out that there are multiple responses to stress. We don't react every time with the fight-or-flight response. We have a choice, and much of the time we choose a very different way to address the events in our life.

Researchers refer to a common and more effective response to stress as the "challenge response." When we see an athlete excel in the most critical moments of the big game, we are watching the challenge response. When the pressure is on in your job and everyone is counting on you and you deliver, you are operating from the challenge response. What I saw on the sailboat that day was everyone operating fully from the challenge response. This motivates us to rise to the occasion, increases our self-confidence, and prompts us to be curious about what else we can learn.

This is not to say that all the individuals I have interviewed or worked with over the last 10 years don't spend ample time in fight-or-flight mode in response to some situations. We all are wonderfully human. The difference is that, time after time, at some point these people decide to run toward the chaos that others are running away from; they are the ones who gather everyone around to say *we are going to make this work.*

Why does purpose help us access the challenge response to stress? The key factor triggering your choice of response is your own internal assessment of your ability—or lack of it—to address the current situation. In other words, if you believe the situation you are facing overwhelms your abilities, you will have a fight-or-flight response. If you believe you can succeed, you will muster a challenge response. The way to turn fight-or-flight into a challenge response is to focus on the resources available that are within your control.

Researchers have found a number of methods that help people shift into the challenge response:

- Recalling similar crucible or difficult experiences that you addressed successfully
- Reminding yourself of the support of people you care about
- Praying, or believing that others are praying for you

We can add another method to the list: "Thinking about or connecting to your purpose." In case after case from my interviews and firsthand observation, when all hell breaks loose, stepping into the room of purpose is a powerful access point to the challenge response of stress. Here are just a few more examples of the kinds of things I hear and witness on a regular basis:

LUCA—To liberate the perfect seagull in me and others.

Thinking about my purpose changes things completely. It changes how I see myself and what actions I take. Do I drop back to my insecurities and fears? Yes, I do. And then I step back into my purpose. It gives me the strength to really lead when I would have micromanaged every-one to death in the past.

JONATHAN—Cracking big solutions for people I care about.

I use my purpose as a resource and ask: How do I live my purpose in this situation? A space that is your own that helps center you.

HANA—Mastering ideas to make beautiful designs.

I lean on my purpose. The default reaction is to throw myself into a million things. Since my purpose is about making beautiful designs, I will step back and do a mind map and plan/design. Stops me from being in panic mode.

DIRK—Race to the unknown—let's find the whistle!

My purpose is fundamentally about taking on stretch challenges. Stepping into the unknown and creating the new. Running into a dark wood determined to find a distant whistle. When working with teams, I like to overcome the anxiety and create alignment of strengths to take the hurdles along the way and get to our destination.

All stress responses are the brain's ways of preparing the body to deal with potential danger. In both the fight-or-flight and the challenge responses, the heart pounds to get the blood coursing through your arteries. Yet, fight-or-flight brings an extra punch by asking our body to produce *more* cortisol. That gives us quick energy but also shuts down our immune system. Add to this cocktail the emotions of anger or fear and things easily escalate.

The challenge response also increases your heart rate, but in this case the speeding pulse makes you feel full of energy. Research shows that none of us are "calm" under pressure when we perform at our best. But in spite of that nervous feeling in our gut when we are in the challenge response, we also feel engaged, clear, and positive about the outcome. We are excited about what can happen and we go for it. So, what happens to the chemical cocktail created when stress hits us? The difference is that during a challenge response the body releases higher levels of DHEA (dehydroepiandrosterone). This hormone gives our brain the ability to learn from stressful encounters and aids post-stress recovery in our body. Therefore, when we respond to stress with the challenge response, we gain the energy we need to overcome the stressor and even benefit from the experience.

Another thing that I see in the executives I work with is a high motivation to connect with and engage others in the larger challenge. Few people tell me about solitary or independent, focused actions. Choosing to bring others along with us in our challenge response triggers the release of another hormone, oxytocin. Some stress researchers refer to oxytocin as the bravery or courage hormone. Scientists have documented that elevated levels of oxytocin

- Increase the desire to connect with others
- Improve the ability to discern what others think and feel

- Increase empathy and intuition
- Increase levels of trust and desire to help significant others
- Decrease fear and the fight-or-flight response

Everyone experiences this occasionally, along with the warm glow also associated with oxytocin. What about the leaders who choose over and over to step further into crazy situations? Research shows that the brain learns from these challenge response situations. The more we experience them, with the help of the DHEA hormone, the faster our brain rewires itself to allow increased levels of the challenge response.

Psychologists call this *stress inoculation*. This helps explain why in professional situations where highly stressful situations are common (emergency rooms, combat, firefighting), the training focuses on repeated practice scenarios that allow participants to step into the challenge response more easily. The more we do it, the more comfortable we become.

For you and me, that means every day is a training day, so to speak.

Transforming fight-or-flight

When we step into our purpose and identify the meaning an experience has for us, no matter how difficult, it changes our relationship to the event. We transition from being stressed out to being purposefully focused.

> MAC—To continue the quest to slay giants
> and change the world.

What if your purpose statement was "To continue the quest to slay giants and change the world"? What do you think your response to stressful situations would be? Let me introduce you to Mac, a leader who has transformed a literal fight-or-flight response into the challenge response to stress.

For Mac, "quest" refers to always experiencing life as a journey as opposed to a destination. You are never done—there is always another giant to be slain. "Slaying giants" comes from a childhood passion for video games and a magical moment of playing the Nintendo game *Punch Out*. By the time he was 12, Mac was so good at boxing Mike Tyson in this game that the whole neighborhood would show up to watch and cheer him on as if it were a live boxing match. Here we have someone whose purpose and childhood memory are all about perseverance, fighting, overcoming obstacles, doing good, and having fun along the way. He has always loved taking on the gnarly challenges that others run away from. "Changing the world" refers to Mac's lifelong desire to make a difference, which he has expressed in roles ranging from a Peace Corps volunteer in Guatemala to his current position at a major foundation's philanthropic global health and development organization.

Mac's childhood was characterized by change, transition, and instability. His mother was 18 when he was born, and his father was a boxer, a professional fighter à la Mike Tyson. His parents divorced when he was young, and he moved around a lot, changing schools, changing neighborhoods, and continually forming new relationships. At the time, he struggled with all the changes, yet now he is most at ease when things are changing around him. Research by Karen Parker at Stanford shows that instead of making us more fragile, early life stresses cause the brain to develop in ways that reduce the fear response, strengthen impulse control, and generate positive motivation. Mac is a good example of that phenomenon. He is always the calmest person in the room. It's no surprise that, along with golf, a passion that has sustained him for many years is boxing. He goes to the gym twice a week and says, "I don't think I could stop doing it." The mental focus and physical discipline of boxing are at his core. His purpose of slaying giants has given him an interesting way to exercise fighting in a way that allows him to change the world instead of getting kicked by it!

Mac loves a hot kitchen. It hasn't always been easy for him to find professional situations that require the extreme level of energy and engagement he thrives in. He says, "The gnarly stuff tends to find you when you don't want to go there, that place nobody wants to go." One of his recent stressful experiences was as part of the foundation's response to the Ebola epidemic in 2014. For months, he worked 12- to 14-hour days, totally energized, motivated, and at his best, serving as the interface between senior leadership, implementation teams, and partners on the ground in West Africa.

Only purpose can turn a metaphor that is literally about fighting into a supercharged challenge response. Yet when the high of the Ebola response efforts were followed by a series of reorganizations and the departure of a boss he had truly enjoyed working for, the fight-or-flight response was running the show. In full flight mode, Mac took his first-ever three-week vacation. While he was on "vacation," he kept reflecting on his purpose.

He realized that he could be a victim of change and keep running, or he could step up to lead and help others. Until then, Mac had always been the good first officer but never the captain. If he stayed at his current organization, he would have to be the captain and fully own a major change effort that would fundamentally alter how the organization operated. The CEO and top team all believed he could do it—but did *he*? He would be front and center, driving transformative changes as the one making it all happen. He reminded himself, "Be yourself, be your best self, be true to who you are."

When we talked before he went on vacation, I sensed his strong desire to just get away and have some time to reflect. I often see this pattern when leaders find themselves being overrun by the fight-or-flight response: they instinctively take a break and give themselves time to reflect and breathe. What we do in those moments reveals our nature and determines our course in life. Do we allow ourselves to be led by our purpose, or do we keep running? Here's what I have noticed across all the people I have interviewed: The more we operate from our purpose, the shorter the cycle time is from fight-or-flight to the challenge response. It's inevitable that we all spend some time in fight-or-flight, but our purpose helps us move beyond it faster.

Over the three weeks, Mac didn't just reflect on his purpose. He went back through the stories of his childhood, his passions, and his crucibles and saw the thread of his purpose running through the tapestry of his life. The alignment across all these stories and experiences changed how he looked at himself.

His identity was no longer being a good first officer; instead, he stepped into his purpose as his leadership identity. From here he could turn and face the future, see where the thread was leading him, and step fully into a visible leadership role that would not have been likely 18 months earlier. *When you are clear on who you are and your overarching purpose, when you have clarity and know which direction you want to go, you can chart a path.* After his break, Mac reported, "The good news is my purpose reset the bar for me. Being grounded in all of that is very centering. I don't know if I would have attacked things the same way without the solid footing I had."

Today Mac is fully in the game, driving a very big agenda as the leader who can. He loves to jolt the system into action. His focus is helping people thrive and be energized. He is clear that the past ways of working must be released to master a new model of operating in the VUCA world. "I don't think everyone is energized by disruptive thinking, yet that is the place we need to be. You can get drawn into the swirl.... I have my purpose to check myself. Am I being true to my purpose? If not, I can reset myself and get back."

Would you like to work for Mac? He is by far one of the nicest and calmest individuals I have ever had the pleasure of knowing. Edgy but not on edge, action-oriented without being dramatic, and energized but not over the top, Mac gets my vote among the thousands I have worked with. Of course, he's not the only beautiful example of choosing the challenge response over fight-or-flight. He just happens to be the one I selected for this chapter.

If he didn't know his purpose, who would Mac be? My sense is that his purpose has always been leading him, but he thinks he probably would have passed up the big leadership job and veered toward another comfortable first-officer type role in a similar organization, in a similar sector. He would never have predicted he'd end up where he is now, but if we have learned one thing in this book it's that our purpose really doesn't care what we want or think; sometimes it has its own plans for us. We just need to listen.

Most of us don't need to go looking for stressful situations in our lives. They seem to be everywhere. Having been in the "transformation" business one way or another for the past 30 years, I've heard a constant drumbeat in every organization I have worked with: "We must learn how to do much more with much less." There is nothing on the horizon that will slow the pace of compacting more responsibility and accountability into fewer people. We live in a world of significant job redundancies, restructurings, and mergers. In some ways, the only thing we have control over is how we deal with the stress, because double-hatting jobs, meetings all over the world, and 24/7 emails and text messages aren't going away anytime soon. The purpose that leads through you is waiting to give you the meaning and confidence in your resources that will transform a constant threat into an opportunity.

In *The Upside of Stress*, Kelly McGonigal brings home the challenge we face today at work by reminding us of research done many years ago that is still highly relevant today. In 1975, Dr. Salvatore Maddi of the University of Chicago convinced

Carl Horn, VP at Illinois Bell Telephone (IBT), to allow his team to follow 430 supervisors, managers, and executives and study their responses to stress. In 1981, the six-year mark in the study, deregulation of the telephone industry hit IBT. The firm did what most firms would do today: IBT cut its workforce of 26,000 by 50 percent within one year!

Today we are familiar with this drill, but it was almost unheard of in 1981. It would have been the first time anyone had experienced such a downsizing. Remember, those were the days when you had a job for life.

Dr. Maddi's study of normal corporate stress in the 1970s turned into much more as he and his team followed the participants during the most stressful work experience imaginable at the time. In fact, they kept following those 430 individuals for 12 years, until 1987, administering annual psychological questionnaires, interviews, performance observations, and even medical examinations.

Approximately two-thirds of the participants demonstrated the fight-or-flight response and suffered from bad performance, depression, burnout, obesity, heart attacks, divorces, and many other harmful symptoms. Yet the other third thrived! Exactly the same situation triggered a completely different response. They remained healthy, vibrant, and excelled in their performance, even if they were let go and had to find new jobs. Maddi's work occurred long before the challenge response label became current; he named what he saw *hardiness*: the courage to grow from stress.

His observations of what differentiated these "hardy" people will seem familiar to you by now. They capture what I have seen take place when purpose leads us. The one-third of the managers at IBT who survived and thrived in these difficult circumstances shared these attitudes:

- Stress is part of the adventure. It's a place of growth and meaning. If there's no stress, no meaning or growth is happening.
- No matter how bad it feels, the world is not coming to an end. Stress is like the weather; it will change if you wait long enough.
- While others run away, staying fully engaged in challenging times is the norm.
- We always have options and resources. In the worst case, if the situation is unchangeable, the ability to find the silver lining always is present: "I am a better person for having faced this."

As McGonigal indicates, "People who held these attitudes responded differently to stress. They were more likely to take action and connect with others during stress. They were less likely to turn hostile or self-defensive. They were also more likely to take care of themselves, physically, emotionally, and spiritually. They built a reserve of strength that supported them in facing the challenges in their lives."

I hope you are beginning to realize that stress isn't all the bad things we have made it out to be. A life of purpose will not be a life without stress. Next time you really feel stressed, check the rearview mirror. Maybe your purpose is smiling back at you.

Points to ponder

Exercise on purpose and stress:

- Find something in your life that is both meaningful and causing you a great deal of stress.
  - Why is the activity, relationship, or project so important to you?
  - What would be the impact if you suddenly lost this source of meaning?
  - How is this connected to your purpose?
- Think about the most purposeful activities you have been involved with in your life.
  - Was there any stress?
  - Compared to other activities that felt less purposeful in your life, how were these experiences of stress different?
  - If you had a chance to do it again, would you? Why?

Chapter 12

IMPACT: CHOOSING THE HARD RIGHT OVER THE EASY WRONG

> Strengthen and increase our admiration for honest dealing and clean thinking, and suffer not our hatred of hypocrisy and pretense ever to diminish. Encourage us in our endeavor to live above the common level of life. Make us to choose the harder right instead of the easier wrong, and never to be content with a half-truth when the whole can be won.
>
> —West Point cadet prayer

I have worked with leaders and executives from almost every field and industry, but one of my most memorable experiences was standing before a faculty group at the United States Military Academy at West Point. About half of the 40 people in the room were career educators and half were active duty officers on a three-year tour that included a top civilian master's program and two or three years of either teaching or being responsible for a company of approximately 130 cadets. Even though their situation was unique in many ways, this group had something in common with every other set of leaders I've stood before: Their purpose had been leading them for a long time, they just didn't know exactly what it was.

Our host, Colonel Tony Burgess—an alumnus of our program

and director of the Army's Center for the Advancement of Leader Development and Organizational Learning—shared the West Point cadet prayer with me and my team. Tony was right—I needed to see this document. One phrase has stayed with me since that day: "to choose the harder right instead of the easier wrong." It exemplifies what it means to fully lead from purpose.

Clarity in the face of the unknown

My conversations and interviews with leaders from all walks of life and all parts of the globe have revealed a surprising common experience. They not only choose the hard rights over the easy wrongs in their journeys, but to a person they do so with deep clarity in the face of the unknown. Clarity of purpose allows them to make important decisions that look risky to others but that make them feel they are "finally home." Few things could be more valuable to leading in today's world than this particular effect of purpose.

Our alumni tell us that the big decisions—the ones for which no real data is available—are the ones where purpose has the biggest impact and provides clarity and confidence. Purpose is like a compass needle that points us toward our deeper truth. As leaders, we spend much of our time simply exercising good management—where what's important is getting all the data and seeing the path that makes the most logical sense. True leading (of both ourselves and others), on the other hand, is about going where no one else has gone. There may not be a path, and we have no historical experience or knowledge to stand on.

One big decision we all make is choosing which profession to take up and which job to accept or decline. Every member of the crew I interviewed at West Point had made a very clear choice early in life, with long-term implications. When you choose the military as a career, you won't make as much money as your peers. In most cases, you won't have much control over your job or your mission. You can't just quit, and you might move every two or three years, with or without your family. If you are "lucky," you get to go on—and return from—a challenging deployment in which injury and death are close at hand. Many of these men and women had been in multiple deployments and some of them had permanent disabilities as a result. Almost all had lost friends.

Most of us have never made such a sacrifice, nor will we, and that's not the point here. If you look at the hardest decisions you have made, did you have all the data? None of us do, but, when it's right, we know. Even when things get crazy, we know if we chose the hard right over the easy wrong!

Each of us can look back on our life and remember the moments when our decisions made a difference for us and those around us. When we choose the hard right, we look deep inside and take the action that honors who we truly are. The easy wrong is never hard to grasp—we think life will be "easier," so to speak. Yet many of us spend our days wishing we had listened to the voice of purpose.

Purpose dramatically increases your ability to "know" what you need to do, especially when the whole world is telling you to do something different.

Doing what doesn't make sense

Most of the things accomplished by the people we admire and respect—the ones we perceive to be "great"—made no sense at the time. When they decided to do it, nobody else thought it was a good idea. What's more, each of these people had a unique gift that we can now easily see. Galileo, Monet, Helen Keller, Mandela, Gandhi, Lincoln, Franklin D. Roosevelt, Rosa Parks, Steve Jobs, Henry Ford...all stepped up against the prevailing worldview and gave us something that made the world better. In our own lives, each of us must face this question down and answer it: What is that "hard right over easy wrong" decision we need to make? What actions do we need to take?

PRERANA ISSAR—To be a catalyst for positive change in the world, especially for women.

Prerana Issar exemplifies choosing the hard right in life. Prerana was deeply unhappy when I met her. Having grown up in India and worked in human resources, she accepted a global role in London with the expectation that she would continue to follow the fast trajectory up through the organization. When her three-year-old daughter asked her why she traveled so much for her job, Prerana wanted to have a more compelling answer than she felt she had then—both for her daughter and for herself. Prerana looked around and found two very interesting opportunities. The most logical choice, a job that would allow her to stay in London, was head of HR in Europe for one of the most famous consumer brands in the world. This would set her up to take a role as head of HR for a large retailer or to return to India in the future. Also, it would please her husband and kids who were happily settled in London.

The other job offer was a huge risk and would mean Prerana and her kids would have to live in Rome, Italy, while her husband commuted from London. The logical job progression Prerana had planned would be sidelined. On top of that, this job would require frequent travel to some of the most dangerous places on the planet. The job was chief human resource officer (CHRO) for the United Nations World Food Programme (WFP). WFP is the world's largest humanitarian agency and provides the food for all United Nations refugee camps around the world, as well as millions of people in war zones and crises who are not refugees. Instead of visiting coffee shops in the trendy parts of Berlin, Paris, and Copenhagen, she would go to South Sudan, Syria, Jordan, Niger, and every other place where the most vulnerable people lived. In 2017, WFP provided $7 billion of food aid, which is 60 percent of the world's food aid.

This HR position came with several unusual responsibilities. There is a plaque on the wall at the World Food Programme headquarters that lists the employees who have died while in the service of the organization. One of Prerana's responsibilities was to reduce the duty of care for WFP employees in harm's way as they tried to feed people in places that were being shelled or where hostage-taking was rampant.

When others pass the buck and hope someone else will do what is needed, time and time again leaders have told me how their purpose clarifies what is right. Nobody tells me that purpose makes life easy—but it does make things clear. Having many sleepless nights and upsetting a great number of people is part of leading from purpose.

Prerana was struggling with which position to take. The corporate job with the global company would make her husband and kids happy and pay her very well. As a mom, she was being tugged to take this job. On the other hand, Prerana was enormously excited about the possibility of bringing her expertise to an organization that did such noble work, even though it would be a very risky move because she had no experience working in the humanitarian sector. Making a list of all the pros and cons wasn't helping her make her decision. Nor was seeking the advice of the people around her.

I asked her a simple question: "If your purpose was making the decision, which job would it take?"

Prerana's purpose is "To be a catalyst for positive change in the world, especially for women." This is a woman who, at age 14, became angry and decided to put up posters challenging the caste system–based law in India. Even more dangerous, she and her friends did this after the official curfew hour. Fortunately, she didn't get caught, but she showed herself to be a person who will risk much for what she thinks is right.

So, when I asked her that question, she smiled because she realized the decision was easy. Eighty percent of the people WFP's serves are women and children. How else could she more fully live her purpose than by leaving corporate life after almost 20 years and jumping into a role at the World Food Programme in Rome?

Going to work for the WFP was a big adjustment. Every day of the first 18 months challenged Prerana with issues she had never faced and with a lack of resources she had never encountered in her corporate roles. When we talked every few months, she seemed to spend the first 10 minutes highlighting how impossible and crazy it was to do the job she knew needed to be done. After that, she would reconnect to the magnificence of this role—the best place for her to live her purpose at this moment.

Prerana's decision meant that she didn't see her husband

very often and her kids didn't see her as much as she would have liked. Purpose isn't about making life easy. A life of meaning and impact is just that, and many times it isn't going to "look" normal. Prerana also faced issues that no one in HR should ever have to deal with, as the Ebola outbreak and the movement of millions of Syrian refugees stretched the WFP and her beyond all the forecasts of what was "expected." WFP was designed to handle one major crisis at a time, and for the last few years the organization has been dealing with five or six at once. Prerana's nickname from her colleagues at the WFP is "Ms. Valiant."

Prerana has no regrets. She is committed to living her purpose "at scale" as she told me. Welcome to leading in this VUCA world of ours.

Choosing the hard right when it counts most

EVERETT SPAIN—Steward my gifts, love and honor God and my family, and elevate the world.

Let's return to West Point. My colleague Everett Spain currently leads the Department of Behavioral Sciences and Leadership at West Point. His journey has been a series of hard rights over easy wrongs. Everett's purpose is "Steward my gifts, love and honor God and my family, and elevate the world."

This is the first time this book has shared a purpose statement that includes the words "God" and "love," so it's worth a short digression. It's interesting how much, all around the world, those two words make people struggle. Each of us has words that have deep significance for us. Most purpose statements that work have words that don't make sense to others. The words "God" and "love" are words that matter most for some of us, and when that is the case we must honor it. Remember, it's not the words themselves that are important, but the meaning they hold for us that is our purpose.

When we worked with the West Point faculty, at first I was surprised that the words "God" and/or "love" were in more than half of their purpose statements. While these words do show up in the corporate world, we find them much less frequently. But if your job includes the possibility of being disabled for life or killed, it makes sense that one or both of those words would be at the heart of your purpose. We would probably see a similar pattern in a group of clergy members. Both professions are in service to a higher calling.

Everett Spain graduated third in his class at West Point and started the traditional climb up the ranks. The 82nd Airborne and Ranger school were just part of his journey. Commands in Kosovo and Europe with a wife and four kids in tow made for a very busy life. One of his biggest hard-right-versus-easy-wrong decisions was to be aide-de-camp to General David Petraeus for 19 months during the Surge in Iraq. He didn't see his family for months on end, and when he did the visits were brief. Purpose isn't always about being comfortable. Everett was on track to become a general when he decided to take a left turn against all the advice he got from the people around him. No, he didn't leave the Army, but to most people it looked like he did. He decided to become an academic and get his PhD in Business Administration and Leadership. This decision meant he would no longer be considered for promotion. Given his current role, we can now look back and say in hindsight that his choice was a good one.

Everett thought long and hard about this choice, but many times choosing the hard right over the easy wrong—a decision that will have an impact on us and others around us—is a choice we must make in the moment. While getting his PhD, Everett decided to train for the Boston Marathon. On April 15, 2013, Everett was running the Boston Marathon, serving as a blind-guide for Steve Sabra, a 58-year-old visually impaired engineer and friend. "They were approximately 100 meters from the finish when the first bomb detonated. Col. Spain pulled Mr. Sabra through the finish and transferred him to another member of the support staff and raced to the site of the first blast to treat the injured. He proceeded to use his shirt as a tourniquet to stem the bleeding of one victim while simultaneously reassuring his frantic daughter. Col. Spain then moved to assist other injured and then to search for victims that might have been trapped or covered by debris; and to evacuate the building which he thought had been set on fire."

In the medical tent, he saw a woman with multiple serious limb injuries and severe burns; she was alone on a gurney, pale and shaking. He covered her with a blanket, then comforted her, holding her hand and reassuring her as he accompanied her in an ambulance to Boston Medical Center.

A year later, with many of the survivors and their families in attendance, Everett Spain received the Soldier's Medal, the U.S. Army's highest award for valor in a noncombat situation. Although he usually avoids the limelight, he was pressed to speak at the ceremony. His comments, excerpted here, show what it is like to live from purpose in a moment of choice.

First, I'm no hero. I'm just a work in progress trying to be a decent husband, father, classmate, colleague, citizen, soldier, and friend, while often falling short.....

No, I am no hero—but I am a soldier. And I know that every service member who has served, or who will serve in the uniform of our nation, as well as their family members, would have done the same thing I did on that day, or more. It is just what we do. Also, numerous others from all walks of life would have done the same, and many did....

Several people have asked me why I ran towards the smoke. That is a difficult question to answer. What I do know is that I have been blessed by the investment others have made in my character development throughout my lifetime.

The Spain Family ran towards the smoke—as a boy, my parents role-modeled how to be an upstander, a person who deliberately stands up for people who are unable to stand up for themselves.

The Boy Scouts ran towards the smoke—they taught me to help others daily.

The Church ran towards the smoke—they taught me to be willing to lay down my life for another.

West Point ran towards the smoke—they taught me selfless service and duty.

Harvard University ran towards the smoke—they expected me to be a leader who makes a difference in this world.

The U.S. Military ran towards the smoke—they taught me to never leave a fallen comrade.

No, I can say with perfect honesty that it wasn't me who ran towards the smoke. But the values deliberately imprinted on me by my faith, my family, my friends, my mentors, and many character-building institutions over time, and our American spirit—those values ran towards the smoke that day.

Finally, I'd like to close with a few observations.

- **Darkness**—I am not sure exactly what that is, but I know it is overcome by light.
- **Fear**—I am not sure exactly what that is, but I know it is overcome by hope.
- **Anger**—I am not sure exactly what that is, but I know it is overcome by forgiveness.
- **Inadequacy**—I am not sure exactly what that is, but I know it is overcome by Grace.
- **Hate**—I am not sure exactly what that is, but I know it is overcome by Love.

Our purpose doesn't usually wait for us to ask, "What action will most be aligned with my purpose in this moment?" Still, even if Everett had not known his purpose, I am sure he would have taken the same actions on that day. His actions are an expression of the purpose that leads through him. Many other people at the finish line that day helped the injured; others did not. I wish I could know each person's purpose and see the impact of purpose on the actions he or she took. Clearly, Everett's profession and experience prepared him to operate from a different mindset than that of most people. If you wanted someone with the right purpose in the right moment at the end of the Boston Marathon, you would be hard-pressed to find anyone whose purpose would be more helpful than Everett's. As I write this, Everett is responsible for developing leadership skills in the 4,000 cadets at West Point. It is an extremely challenging and important job that requires Everett to step in and lead from his purpose every day.

The stories in this chapter, especially Everett's, pose the question: Is there a link between courage and purpose? Clearly, Everett demonstrated and was honored for his perceived courage in a moment when others were running away from the blast site. Remember, at the time no one knew how many other bombs might go off. Thank goodness, we don't see events like this often. Philosopher Daniel Putman offers descriptions of three types of courage:

- **Physical courage:** A selfless act in the face of risk to one's own physical well-being. Everett's actions are an example of this kind of courage. This was the only version of courage I believed there was until recently.
- **Moral courage:** Doing what is ethically right in the face of significant negative social consequences. Corporate and government whistleblowers who do the right thing without regard to the reaction of their peers exhibit moral courage. I haven't had the privilege of seeing this up close; I would find it interesting to interview these individuals to learn the connection between their actions and their purpose.
- **Psychological courage:** Action taken despite the internal fear of being rejected or humiliated, or of failing badly. Prerana's decision to leave the predictable corporate HR track

and jump into being the head of HR for the World Food Programme is a compelling example of this type of courage. Nic Brassey's story (chapter 10) of running a full-day session for 400 employees, in Dutch, after only six months of lessons, probably makes many of us pause. And, yes, most of us can relate to the feelings we have before a big presentation requiring this type of courage.

Psychological courage is the kind of courage I had seen *all the time* with our program participants. We all have fears in our lives, and many of them make no sense, given the external success that others perceive in us. We ask a question early in our programs: "What is the part of you most people don't see that is a key part of who you are?" In response, we hear the full range of fears that we all live with that others don't see. One of the most common fears is "the imposter syndrome"—the fear that, at any moment, someone will come up to you and say, "You don't really belong here." From the outside no one imagines that many if not most of the executives I have worked with feel this way. They are highly productive and capable people. Yet, I repeatedly hear different versions of that story. We all must choose whether we are going to let our fears run us or follow our purpose. In the stories people share about leading from their purpose, it's clear that purpose doesn't take away the fear; it just helps us act despite the fear. If all we have is the fear, then fear wins. But if we have a sense of our deeper purpose, we can "make it so." Prerana had the psychological courage to step into a job that had none of the trappings or future opportunities that her career up to that moment defined as success. Over the next four years, she faced the most challenging demands in the history of the World Food Programme, from the Ebola outbreak to the civil war in Syria, and more.

Defining courage

What is courage? For most of us, courage, no matter how we define it, feels like it belongs to someone else. We rarely feel we are courageous. It's those around us who say, "Wow—that took courage!" and our response is usually, "No, I was just doing what seemed natural," or, "If you knew how scared I was when I did that you wouldn't think that was courage!" The person who responds, "Yep, I am one courageous dude!" is someone you should run away from!

Since the days of Aristotle and Plato, philosophers have been talking about courage, yet only recently is a clear definition emerging. Christopher R. Rate has spent much of his academic career attempting to do just that—create a common understanding of courage by looking at all the definitions and many examples, as well as working with a research team on a series of studies on how we see courage in our day-to-day life. The team's results offer not a definition per se, but more a list of the key characteristics of courage, those that were common to all the definitions and examples of courage he studied:

- The action is freely chosen.
- The act is attempted or accomplished at substantial risk or danger to the individual.
- The individual seeks to bring about a noble or worthy purpose (something that matters is at stake).

If we combine Putman's "psychological courage" with these characteristics, we find ourselves in the world that you and I deal with daily. We each have the opportunity to choose actions that we perceive as being high-risk yet are deep expressions of our purpose. Knowing our purpose gives us the ability to see the choices between our own hard rights and easy wrongs more clearly.

We have all made lists of tradeoffs—pluses and minuses that rarely measure up to the dimensions of the choice we must make. Choices aren't made in the rational world of pros and cons. The root of the word *courage* is *cor*, the Latin word for *heart*. If only our head is involved in the decision, no courage occurred. Courage shows up when our heart is in the game, and our heart knows what matters.

When did you last say or do something risky because of something that really mattered? We have our values, yet what is the catalyst to act? All my discussions with leaders convince me that purpose is leading us, and looking at the times that we have acted with courage is a good way to get clarity on purpose. Purpose will get involved in the discussion between our heart and our head, showing us the answer that usually feels the most risky and scary. In that moment, we must choose. Sometimes, in hindsight, we know we should have listened to "that voice." The true gift we can offer ourselves is to make every day a day of demonstrating our own courage to ourselves. The best path is the one that others can't see, but as we follow it we know just how much we had to honor our purpose in order to do what we did each day.

Next, we step into the impact of purpose on happiness. As we have learned how purpose connects us to our courage, is there room to be happy as well?

Points to ponder

1. When in the past have you chosen the easy wrong as opposed to the hard right? What do you wish you had done differently?
2. What is the easy wrong others would like you to choose?
3. When in the past did you do the hard right, and what was the impact over time? How do you know it was the hard right?
4. What is the hard right that is facing you right now that you would rather postpone?
5. What does your desire to take the hard right say about who you are and what purpose may be leading you?
6. When have you "run toward the smoke" as opposed to away from it, as Everett did? Why did you do it?
7. When did you last take a risk because of something important? What does this begin to say about the unique gift you bring to the world, your purpose?

Chapter 13

IMPACT: PURPOSE AND HAPPINESS

> This is the true joy in life, the being used for a purpose
> recognised by yourself as a mighty one; the being
> thoroughly worn out before you are thrown on the
> rubbish heap; the being a force of Nature...instead of
> a feverish, selfish little clod of ailments and grievances
> complaining that the world will not devote itself to
> making you happy.
>
> —George Bernard Shaw

These words encapsulate the challenge that leading from our purpose brings to our desire to live a happy life. We live in a world that is obsessed with happiness. Happiness has become an industry in itself—a search on Amazon.com yields more than a hundred thousand books related to happiness.

Purpose, meaning, and happiness

Most people assume that having your purpose clear and living it must make you happy. But here is the odd thing: Your purpose will drive you to delay being happy, leading you instead to create something that matters and has deep meaning for you.

We all live with an inner tension caused by the knowledge that the things that make us happy in the moment may not actually make a positive difference in the world. In the previous chapter we talked about choosing the hard right over the easy wrong. You could say that this chapter explains why some things are "hard rights" and others are "easy wrongs." The "hard right" tends to be more purposeful. The core question is, do we focus on leading from our purpose or do we focus on being happy? They have very different consequences.

Purpose is like a pair of glasses that we look through to create meaning in our life. Sometimes, that also creates happiness. Or, as Viktor Frankl, whose book *Man's Search for Meaning* is a must-read for any of us who want to understand what a life of meaning and purpose can bring, says, "Happiness must happen, and the same holds for success: you have to let it happen by not caring about it."

One arena that highlights for some of us the tension between being happy and doing work that brings us meaning is parenthood. Whether or not you have kids, I hope you can appreciate the metaphor. Researchers have studied the connections between having children and happiness. For example, economist Andrew Oswald examined tens of thousands of couples both with and without children to explore the effects of parenting on parents. In her article "All Joy and No Fun," for *New York Magazine*, writer Jennifer Senior recounts her conversation with Oswald:

> [Oswald] is at least inclined to view his data in a more positive light: "The broad message is not that children make you less happy; it's just that children don't make you *more* happy." That is, he tells me, unless you have

more than one. "Then the studies show a more negative impact."

Jennifer Senior's book by the same name, *All the Joy and No Fun—The Paradox of Modern Parenthood*, is a great read if you want to dig deeper into what our kids do to us. In wonderful detail, she delves into the studies of the realities of parenting and how it has dramatically changed in the last hundred years. Reading her work reminds me of my then–13-year-old daughter Keely: every week, when I took her out to a restaurant, she blasted me for the first five minutes and then turned into a normal human being. Or I remember the awful call from my ex-wife telling me that our other daughter, Renee, had been involved in a car accident in which her best friend had died. Or I flash back to the sailing vacation that was anything but a vacation for anyone on the boat (lots of yelling and crying on a sailboat is *not* a vacation), or the family trip in Scotland when I pulled the car over in the middle of nowhere, got out, and started walking back to Boston. The girls still laugh when they tell that story. I wouldn't trade those adventures for anything.

If you are a parent, you have your own list of adventures, joys, and sorrows. The deep sense of meaning and satisfaction that comes from watching those little beings become adults is priceless. I never felt that there were good years or bad years—all of them were amazing (and crazy-making!) in their own way. As Jennifer Senior concludes, "Technically, if parenting makes you unhappy, you should feel better if you're spared the task of doing it. But if happiness is measured by our own sense of agency and meaning, then noncustodial parents lose. They're robbed of something that gives purpose and reward."

Leading from your purpose is a lot like raising kids. It's hard work at times, and, in the moment, we choose not to do what would make us happy right now for the sake of doing the thing that will have greater meaning. Whether it is going to a school play when we are jet-lagged, or driving our kids to a slew of sports events that run together, or calmly sitting them down when we have found a bag of something that smells like oregano while cleaning up their room, we don't do it to be happy but because it matters.

The good news: Purpose can lead to deep fulfillment

When we lead from purpose we are in service to something larger than ourselves. We will delay gratification, happiness, and sleep, because the more purposeful action has a deeper impact that won't let us go. Like parenting, our purpose allows us to step into very challenging situations and persist. Much of the time, being "happy" is *not* what this feels like, yet there is a deep level of fulfillment as we look back at what we have participated in creating.

RYAN WHITLOW—Be a tour guide in life, telling stories that matter, walking alongside and pointing out things of interest. You can decide for yourself if you want to take a picture.

Ryan Whitlow's purpose statement perfectly captures choosing the journey to what matters over what makes us happy: "Be a tour guide in life, telling stories that matter, walking alongside and pointing out things of interest. You can decide for yourself if you want to take a picture." Ryan is a world-class storyteller. He thinks in stories. His view is that he has a dual responsibility of experiencing life and telling about it.

Telling stories is Ryan's craft, and he has many stories about how he applies his purpose at work as a head of leadership development, yet his personal stories are the ones that capture the tension between purpose and happiness. He didn't want to tell me a story from his professional life. No, he had to tell me a story that made us both cry. His purpose had prepared him for something that matters much more than simply being happy.

Ryan's most cherished—and most challenging—relationship was with his daughter, Ashley. Ashley was severely mentally handicapped, and her physical challenges included a tracheotomy feeding tube. According to the doctors, her life expectancy was only six to nine years. Probably his greatest teacher in life was the journey to help his daughter learn how to do things she didn't think she could do. But as Ashley grew up, Ryan and his wife reached the limits of what they could do 24/7. No amount of love would make up for the physical and psychological care his daughter needed. "The most gut-wrenching moment was when my Ashley couldn't live at our house and she had to go to a special needs facility," he recalls. As Ryan told this story, we were both holding back tears. As a parent, I just can't imagine what it would be like to be in his shoes.

A few years later, Ashley passed away at 27. Yes, you could say that Ryan's purpose wasn't front and center in this part of his story. How could taking his daughter to a state institution and having her pass away be anything other than just a sad and painful story? But this isn't the end of the story.

Purpose has its own timing and knocks on our door uninvited. When you have a special needs child, like Ashley, you get to know all the other parents in similar circumstances. Ryan educated me about the societal problem of special needs children becoming adults when the custodial parents are too old to care for them. Facilities like the one where Ashley lived become critical to allowing everyone to live in an honorable way.

Two years after Ashley's death, out of the blue, Ryan received a call from the parents whose children were still at the facility. The state had decided to close it. All the parents had congregated to figure out how best to get the state to keep it open. They "decided" that Ryan should talk to the state legislature and convince them. Ryan, who was struggling with having lost Ashley, didn't want to go back and reopen all the parts of this journey. Whether or not you have kids, you can understand Ryan's reaction to this unwanted request. Yet, many times purpose doesn't care about what will bring us happiness in the moment; it calls us to do what matters.

Ryan decided to have a chat with Ashley. "So, I went to her grave and said, 'What do you want me to do here?' What came back was 'What is your purpose?'...Be a tour guide....These politicians had no idea what it was like to be responsible for a disabled child. I went to the governor and legislature and I told them my story: 'I am here to describe how you help a disabled child and what it is like to be afraid. We are afraid of neglect, abuse, and lack of help.' I found such power in telling my story."

Purpose is a powerful thing when you listen to it. It will have you do things you would never imagine or decide to do if your goal was to be happy. We can argue as much as we want about who was "talking" to Ryan that day in front of his daughter's grave. What's important is how purpose got Ryan to put aside some of the most challenging emotions any parent can have and live his purpose in a way that others could benefit from his journey.

I wish that this story had a happy ending and the legislature decided to keep the institution open, but that's not the way things turned out. Sometimes it's when the world doesn't follow us and we live our purpose anyway that it has the most "impact" on us. We are leading in those moments.

When things really don't go as planned

**DOLF—Be the gardener with boundless curious energy
to grow a better world.**

There is the plan and then there is the reality of what happens. Dolf's purpose is "Be the gardener with boundless curious energy to grow a better world." Dolf has had a green thumb all his life. As a kid, he was always growing things and used to take care of the neighbors' gardens. Even as an adult he spent hours every weekend maintaining his rooftop garden and months nurturing an avocado seed to get it to sprout. You might think that life would be nice and easy for a smart Dutch kid selling beer. Yet, his purpose had a different plan. In the mid-2000s, early in his career, he received a big promotion and assignment in the Congo. If you want happiness, you should go someplace else... but if you want to do something that matters, here we go!

> The Congo is an extreme business environment. On the one side, you must hit your numbers, you must make your plans—you behave as if you are working for any

other big, fast-moving consumer operation. But you're in a bizarre business environment. You carry responsibility for the well-being of your employees far beyond what you would under normal circumstances. The Democratic Republic of the Congo is a challenging place from any perspective. On the United Nations Human Development Index, Congo is in the bottom five for poverty. It is the worst place in the world on the Ease to Do Business ranking. Being relatively young to the position in such an environment was an incredible stretch for me.

After years of civil war, DRC was finally stabilizing with the help of the international community and planned the first democratic elections in 2006. Also, our business had gone through endless turbulence and was not in a healthy shape. There was renewed hope for the country and we were trying to do our part. Here I was with my wife and two young kids living in a place coming out of endless conflict and where things could turn nasty any minute.

In gardening, what you love most is the plant that you find and bring back to life, not the one that just grows perfect from the first days of being watered. Here I needed to diligently and compassionately rebuild the confidence of the local employees who had gone through endless personal and professional troubles. We weren't just selling beer, but rather we were trying to improve the lives of everyone, from the team and their families to the store owner who could have a viable business. As confidence and self-respect returned, we started to get amazing business growth in a place that hadn't seen growth for years.

Finally, it seemed the threat of a civil war was over. The 2006 elections took place in a relatively peaceful way and a new normal settled in. Early 2007 my boss went on vacation and I was replacing him temporarily, responsible for all our people. We also had 30 expatriates, including wives and children, on site. Early one morning the head of security walked into my office and said things didn't feel right. In his view the situation was ripe for violent conflict between the government forces and the militia of the opposition leader. We pulled all the kids out of the international school that morning, creating enormous upset from the school director. But within hours the fighting started with gunfire in the distance. We decided to immediately send our employees home, just keeping a minimal team running some continuous processes at the brewery. We also decided to bring the expat families to my house and my neighbor's house, which were next to the brewery, as it was too late to evacuate. For two days the fighting was all around the brewery. A couple of missiles fell on the brewery but luckily we suffered nothing but material damage. Soldiers on both sides fired bullets up into the air that would come down without warning and come through the roof.

Our employees in the township were disconnected from TV and radio and were not aware of what was happening at the brewery. A small group came to the brewery on the morning after the violence started; they found the brewery gates closed and were caught in the crossfire. The security manager called and told me there were

10 people who wanted access to the brewery and asked what he should do. I asked, "What's your security advice? Can you open the gate?" And he said, "No, I wouldn't. I cannot check whether there's half an army behind them who could get access to the brewery at the same time where we still have around a hundred employees on the inside."

I asked what would happen to the people. He said that their lives would be in jeopardy. I had about 10 seconds to decide. It's not a typical business decision! Nobody prepares you for this. I decided that they could not have access to the brewery through that gate, but we would open another gate to an area where there were only materials and no people. But there were a couple of hundred meters to cover between the two gates. Half the employees made it to the other gate. By sheer luck, nobody got killed or injured. A couple of weeks later, it hit me—what if someone had been seriously hurt or even killed?

Eventually, the fighting ended with almost one thousand people killed in Kinshasa.

I don't know about you, but I am not hearing a lot of happiness in Dolf's story. A huge sense of relief and satisfaction that no one was killed, yes. Let's hope that none of us experience anything similar. Yet we have all had our purpose get us into situations that are wildly stressful adventures. When you are at peace with who you are, there is a level of satisfaction that is bigger than the momentary "happiness" everyone is chasing but can't find. Who would Ryan or Dolf be today if they had not faced these crucible experiences? Their purpose helps them understand why they have done what they did and why it makes sense and matters. We all desire a happy life, but what makes us come alive is a life of purpose.

Drilling down on happiness and meaning

A research paper from Stanford Business School, titled "Some Key Differences between a Happy Life and a Meaningful Life," delineates the dilemma and opportunity we face in living our purpose instead of chasing the fickle flame of happiness. Like you, I want a happy life, yet a great deal of what the world gives me is a paradox at best. Neither Ryan nor Dolf chose the situations they found themselves in. None of us do. The only choice we have is what we do while in a situation. When everything is stripped away, our purpose leads us through.

The researchers conclude, "The unhappy but meaningful life is seriously involved in difficult undertakings. It was marked by ample worry, stress, argument, and anxiety. People with such lives spend much time thinking about past and future. They expect to do a lot of deep thinking, they imagined future events, and they reflect on past struggles and challenges."

A happy life without purpose is possible, but it comes with a couple of caveats. It "characterizes a relatively shallow, self-absorbed, or even selfish life, in which things go well, needs and desires are easily satisfied, and difficult or taxing entanglements are avoided."

Sounds like a great place to go for vacation but I'm not sure I would want to live there.

Luckily, a purposeful life isn't necessarily an unhappy one, and purpose and happiness do feed off each other much of the time, but they have very different roots. According to Aristotle, there are two ways to pursue happiness. The first is a eudaemonic life in which we are in harmony with our inner spirit (purpose); the other is a hedonic life aimed at positive, in the present moment, self-centered experiences. Aristotle was very clear that the eudaemonic path was the better of the two. In his view this was a path that appeared over the course of one's whole life. The full enrichment of a human life was the desired outcome. Thus, we are required to make hard choices between the greater good and more immediate pleasures and temptations; this often includes sacrifice and challenge. Aristotle believed we should experience both eudaemonic and hedonic pleasures but be mindful of the weight we give each.

We can find a good example of what I believe Aristotle is talking about in Angela Duckworth's research on grit. Here is how she defines *grit*:

> Why were the highly accomplished so dogged in their pursuits? For most, there was no realistic expectation of ever catching up to their ambitions. In their own eyes, they were never good enough. They were the opposite of complacent. And yet, in a very real sense, they were satisfied being unsatisfied. Each was chasing something of unparalleled interest and importance, and it was the chase—as much as the capture—that was gratifying. Even if some of the things they had to do were boring, or frustrating, or even painful, they wouldn't dream of

giving up. Their passion was enduring. In sum, no matter the domain, the highly successful had a kind of ferocious determination that played out in two ways. First, these exemplars were unusually resilient and hardworking. Second, they knew in a very, very deep way what it was they wanted. They not only had determination, they had direction. It was this combination of passion and perseverance that made high achievers special. In a word, they had grit.

A professor and MacArthur genius grant winner, Duckworth wanted to understand the underlying connection between grit and its role in purpose as opposed to pleasure. She doesn't do things small, so she asked 16,000 American adults to complete the Grit Scale and a supplementary questionnaire that probed how important purpose or pleasure were as motivators for the participants. What she discovered is that those people who were the most "gritty" in their journey were also clear about their purpose. "Higher scores on purpose correlate with higher scores on the Grit Scale."

Thus, leading from purpose as opposed to choosing the thing that will make you happy have very different impacts on where we end up in our journey. All things worth doing require significant amounts of determination, effort, and commitment.

Our purpose allows us to see the thread of who we are and where we are going as it weaves through the fabric of our life story. Therefore, it helps us to integrate the past with the present and the future. It makes clear the deeper meaning of why we are here and brings the invitation to step up and live from

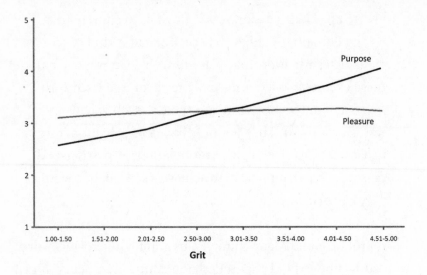

our purpose fully, as Ryan and Dolf demonstrate. Purpose will stick with you when all hell breaks loose as well as when you are happy. Happiness, on the other hand, is a subjective feeling that occurs in the moment. Happiness is tangible, real, wonderful, and fickle for most of us. Would you pick a life of purpose in which happiness just "happens," or a life pursuing happiness with little or no purpose?

Making your choice

Don't get me wrong. Living your purpose isn't all about sacrifice and unhappiness. But there are many differences between pursuing happiness and leading from purpose.

Pursuing happiness	Leading from purpose
Is focused on having one's needs and desires satisfied, including being free of unpleasant experiences.	Forfeits some pleasant things in life for what needs to happen
Is about feeling good in the present	Allows us to integrate the past, present, and future, and see the deeper meaning of the path we are on
Is about achieving momentary happiness	Points the way to long-term fulfillment
Is hard to maintain over an extended period of time	Sets a course that doesn't change
Is mainly about getting what one wants and needs, including from other people or even just by using money	Brings our unique lens and gift to those we desire to serve (including ourselves)

The good news is that a life of purpose, while perhaps not as "happy" as one focused on short-term pleasure, may be much more satisfying to you and the ones you lead. What if the contentment and satisfaction we experience when we allow ourselves to be led by purpose is actually a deeper, more resilient form of happiness?

Points to ponder

1. What are some of the most meaningful moments in your career and life?
2. Which of these moments required you to delay or forfeit being happy to create the meaningful moment?
3. Where do you find yourself on the priority of pleasure versus a purposeful life?
4. Where do you most need to lead from purpose?

IMPACT: SAVING THE WORLD, SAVING YOURSELF

> BILL MOYERS: Unlike the classical heroes, we're not going on our journey to save the world, but to save ourselves.
>
> JOSEPH CAMPBELL: And in doing that, you save the world.
>
> —*Joseph Campbell and the Power of Myth,*
> June 21, 1988

Many of the leaders I work with have one big fear in common: "If I discover my purpose, will I have to quit my job, move to a third world country, and feed the poor?" Like many people, they confuse the power of purpose with having passion for a *cause*. Remember, a cause such as ending hunger or poverty is noble, but it is only a strategy through which we live our purpose. Our purpose is with us no matter where we are and what we are doing. You can be a banker, a marketer, a salesman, or follow any other profession and lead from purpose.

Yet the belief that if you aren't saving the world you are not leading from your purpose is persistent. Much has been written about the perceived link between living your purpose and making a difference in the world. Many authors have even defined purpose as "how you make the world a better place."

Why do so many equate purpose with saving the world? As I have watched many leaders step into their purpose, I have observed that, once they get clarity about the purpose that is leading them, most people have a strong wish to experience it more fully. In the same way actors need a stage and an audience, we need the world as a stage on which to express and experience our purpose. Purpose is that unique gift we bring to the world—and sometimes we end up saving part of it as well.

JEROEN—Never waste the talent.

Jeroen Wels's purpose statement, "Never waste the talent," comes from a magical moment in his childhood. When he was about 12, he realized that he was much smarter than many of the other kids at school. One of his options would have been to not work very hard and just get by. He asked his father what he should do. His father said, "Because you can, don't waste it."

On the surface this message sounds a bit self-absorbed. Basically, you're smart, work hard, and never look back. Yet, the effect for Jeroen of reconnecting to this moment and its impact was quite the opposite.

A more accurate expression of Jeroen's purpose might be "never waste anyone's talent." His early life drive to be his best and his resulting success turned him into a person who had a deep passion to help everyone around him not waste their own talent. In this pursuit, Jeroen went so far as to study for a master's degree in public administration.

As he tells it, "I have the desire to make a difference and a hell of a lot of energy for the deep conversations that can create a breakthrough that allows someone to discover what they are really good at. When someone is having a tough time, I help them get over the hump. I want them to have the clarity for themselves, and then I can move on. If I can use my talents to help others access their talents, I really get excited. I struggle when I see people focusing just on themselves; I see it as a waste of talent. When I discovered my purpose, it dramatically expanded my thoughts of how I wanted to bring it to the world around me. I stepped out and took on a board role for an NGO, contributing back to society."

Being on the board of an NGO is not necessary for Jeroen to operate from his purpose. Yet purpose is always tempting us to expand the impact we can make. On the home front, Jeroen and his wife were foster parents to an Afghan refugee girl for a few years. She is now old enough to live on her own but keeps in regular contact with the Welses as she deals with the challenges of life. No matter what Jeroen is doing, what's clear is that the more he owns his purpose, the more it has become how he interacts with the world.

Taking flight as Buzz Lightyear

TODD TILLEMANS—To be Buzz Lightyear, inspiring others to know no bounds, take bold action, and achieve great things.

I have been looking forward to sharing this next example with you. Todd Tillemans's purpose is "To be Buzz Lightyear, inspiring others to know no bounds, take bold action, and achieve great things." When Todd first shared his purpose in front of a room of about 30 executives, they practically fell of out of their chairs laughing: Todd is built just like Buzz Lightyear, sounds just like him, and has the same boundless energy. (Sometimes I wonder if the Pixar crew based the character on Todd!)

Todd is a big energy executive whose presence fills the room; he loves to double revenue and leave the competition in the dust. During college, he sold advertising for a student newspaper that was in financial trouble. What would Buzz Lightyear do in this situation? Exactly. He took over the paper, cut costs, increased revenue, and—*boom!*—created a very profitable newspaper. Fast-forward to 2003 when he took over another struggling business. This one was at $325 million in revenue and flat in market share. In less than three years he rocketed the business from 28 percent to 41 percent market share and doubled the revenue to $650 million. He pushed in every area to cut costs, double output, and knock the competition out in the process. "Push, Push, Push" is a phrase you'll hear him say, a lot.

What does Buzz Lightyear do when he goes to Russia? He does his due diligence and realizes that the competition is remarkable. The more he digs down, the better they look. The solution? Simple: Acquire them and run it!

You're probably wondering why we feature Todd in this chapter. Clearly, his story fits in the chapter on business growth.

To understand, we must go back to when Todd was seven years old and his parents divorced. He and his mom ended up living on food stamps and public assistance. To go from having everything to having nothing is an unforgettable lesson for any of us. At the age of seven, Todd stepped into being someone who always looks at each challenge as a half-full as opposed to a half-empty reality. For Todd, his crucible story is integral to seeing his purpose as not just about hitting the numbers but also about helping take care of those who might be in a challenging moment in their lives.

When Todd's daughter was six years old she was admitted to Chicago Lurie Children's Hospital for surgery. She needed very advanced care and over time was able to return to full health. Many parents go through Lurie Children's Hospital with their children. Todd witnessed a great many kids who reminded him of himself at seven years old. What does Buzz Lightyear do?

Todd joined the board of Lurie Children's Hospital and worked with others to raise money. Their six-year fund-raising efforts resulted in a new, state-of-the-art, 23-story hospital. This isn't just any hospital; they partnered with 20 cultural institutions in Chicago to create an environment conducive to healing. What happens when your purpose becomes a reality? Where else could Buzz Lightyear be of more service to the world than at a children's hospital? Being "the toy that helps heal kids" is a powerful way to experience his purpose.

What does Todd do today? Currently he is U.S. president at the Hershey Company. Not a bad place for Buzz Lightyear to hang out!

Helping others, helping ourselves

Throughout this book we have met people who have had an impact on the world. But people like Prerana Issar, who took a job at the World Food Programme, or Everett Spain, who was a first responder at the Boston Marathon bombing, are rare. Most of us are in professions and roles that don't have that obvious, "sexy" connection to saving the world. The notion that we are leading from our purpose only when we are busy saving the world excludes about 99 percent of leaders. Jeroen, Todd, and most others in this book have normal jobs, like most of us. They, along with many others, have expanded their impact beyond their day jobs. Why?

To begin with, how on earth do they even find the time and energy? There is a fair amount of research on this that is helpful to those of us who must hold a day job that really doesn't directly "save the world," those who feel that there is not enough time to get everything done at work, let's not even talk about a volunteer role. We have all been there when it feels like there is way too much to do and not enough time in the day to get it done.

Common sense would tell you that the most helpful thing would be a windfall of free time, but this turns out not to be true. According to a Wharton Business School study, the best way to experience a reduction in perceived time scarcity is to *spend time helping someone else.*

What is going on? It turns out that helping others helps us. It makes us feel more competent and capable, like getting a boost of energy that we can then use to deal with our own challenges. As I see it, when we help others we connect to our purpose more easily; it becomes a virtuous cycle. The more we see the impact of our purpose with others, the more energy we get, and that cycle repeats.

As we have learned, meaning and purpose are bedfellows.

Purpose is our unique lens by which we create meaning. There has been a lot of research on what creates meaning at work.

Catherine Bailey, with whom I have had the pleasure of talking a number of times, coauthored an excellent article in *Sloan Management Review*, titled "What Makes Work Meaningful— or Meaningless." The researchers interviewed 135 people from 10 professions in a variety of fields: retail assistants, clergy from various denominations, artists (including musicians, writers, and actors), lawyers, academics from science disciplines, entrepreneurs, nurses in an acute-care hospital, soldiers, conservation stonemasons preserving an ancient cathedral, and garbage collectors. It would be hard to come up with a more diverse group of professions (maybe the guy I worked with who was responsible for Jiffy Peanut Butter would have completed the mix). The authors looked at what created or reduced the sense of meaningfulness these people had in their jobs. So, what did they discover?

The study showed that a key access point to meaning is being in direct contact with others who benefit from our work. Of the professionals studied, those in the "caring" occupations—such as nurses and clergy—had the greatest sense of meaning. Why? Because of the regular contact with those who benefited from their work "at times of greatest vulnerability in their lives."

These are just two of a great number of studies undertaken in completely different situations and all finding the same common thread: If you want to feel more capable, more connected to purpose and meaning, the fastest and best way to do it is to help someone. The key is to have direct contact with that person.

The challenge for most of us is that we don't often see the direct impact of our work on others. Dealing with head count, business forecasts, talent reviews, budget meetings, and so forth provides little opportunity to see the direct impact of our unique gift. So many executives wish for the days when they had direct engagement with clients and front-line employees.

One reason many executives I work with, like Jeroen and Todd, take up "save the world" activities is that they can more directly see the impact of leading from their purpose in those "extracurricular" activities. Helping others in a way in which we immediately see the impact is a core human desire. When we step fully into leading from our purpose, the "little me" inside of all of us disappears. Something bigger becomes present. How we best experience it is when we give it away and see the echo of our purpose in those we help or serve.

Monica Worline is an organizational psychologist at the University of Michigan's Center for Positive Organizations. She has spent her career studying how we create meaning and connection in the workplace. She has created a great exercise that helps us step into having better experiences helping and serving others without changing what we do.

First, think about your current job description (gold star for you if you can find it or remember what it says). If you do find it, you will probably see a list of key tasks, skills required, and the focus of the job. Answer the following questions:

- What if you described your job from the point of view of the people you work with or serve?
- What would they say about how your role helps them?
- How does your job support the greater mission of the organization or the welfare of people in your community?

This exercise has a reliable effect of increasing the sense of meaning and purpose people feel—while changing *nothing* in the job. Remember that purpose is a lens by which we see the world and the meaning we make out of it. Just think what happens when you do this exercise from the perspective of the purpose that is leading you!

Saving yourself to save the world

Yet there is a big problem with saving the world. I have seen it over and over again in the people I have worked with. Associating purpose with making the world a better place or even saving it is an exquisite trap. Yes, everyone tends to move toward applying their purpose to the world around them. Unfortunately, this only works over time if you get one thing right. That one thing is difficult to do and most of us are not good at doing it.

We've all sat through the flight attendants' explanation of oxygen masks. The fact is that when most of us get clarity of our purpose, we take the oxygen mask of purpose and help *everyone else* put it on. As we know from the airline safety instructions we get on every flight we take, we are supposed to put the oxygen mask on *ourselves* first before helping everyone else. The most important thing we need to do with our purpose is apply it to ourselves.

Let's return to Prerana Issar. I shared her story of going to work as the chief human resource officer for the World Food Programme, the United Nations agency focused on food for all who are hungry in the world, including all the world's refugees. The HR function encompasses 450 people across 80 countries.

For the last four years, Prerana led the first organization-wide transformation (people, performance, regulatory framework, culture) in the history of the organization. Over this time she also achieved a remarkable increase in the number of women hired and in key leadership positions, thereby adding significantly to the small pool of women humanitarian leaders. If that wasn't enough, she also kicked off a leadership program for the top 1,000 leaders who deliver most of the world's lifesaving humanitarian response.

It would be hard to find a stronger example of "purpose equals saving the world." More than most of us, Prerana has spent time face-to-face with the people she helps, whether UN World Food Programme staff (she has met 40 percent of them face-to-face in the countries where they work) or the most vulnerable people in the world, whom WFP serves. She has told me about conversations with women and children in South Sudan as inspiring WFP staff handed them food, or discussions with an employee in Liberia (a single mother) about providing food assistance during an Ebola outbreak and her risking her life for her community. Prerana has spent time at nutrition camps in rural Niger, food distribution sites in Syria, and school meal programs for children who will only eat that one meal all day in Sierra Leone. Thus, she had the gift of direct contact on a regular basis with those who were most helped by her work, even while dealing with an organization that was internally complex and slow-moving.

Yet, for the last year of this intense job our conversations went like this.

Nick: "Tell me, how you have been leading from your purpose in the last three months?"

Prerana: "Well, I changed key policies that hadn't been changed for the last 30 years to help WFP be more agile; created and presented the two-year vision and strategic plan that was a success; visited Ethiopia, Niger, and Kenya; and somehow also am juggling being the primary parent for our two kids."

Nick: "So how are you feeling at this moment about what you are up to now?"

Prerana: "I feel proud of what we have achieved—my team and I. But it has come at a cost to me. My back is killing me, and it seems to only be getting worse, I am not home that much, and my kids just want their mom. I am heading for a burnout."

Here things get interesting: We have someone who is saving the world, literally, and it's just not working for her. The key word is *burnout*. I hear that word a lot.

Prerana Issar's purpose is "To be a catalyst for positive change in the world, especially for women." There's just one problem: She left out applying it to the one woman who has to live this purpose, herself. How do we give ourselves what is so powerful to give to others, our purpose?

Most of the executives I have worked with are brilliant at saving the world around them. They got to where they are by serving the organization, their boss, their peers, and their team. Everyone around them believes they are an excellent expression of their purpose. The only thing missing in the equation is themselves. They have left themselves out of their purpose.

When we apply our purpose to ourselves we finally come home, and we finally are able to lead from our purpose at a level of congruency that is most compelling. Everyone around us sees it and can begin to breathe as well. The system won't take care of you. You need to take care of yourself. Purpose will help you do that if you let it.

In Prerana's case, at the end of four years she was completely exhausted. Yet many of the initiatives she had started needed her to stay on if they were to be fully implemented. Should she stay in the role for a few more years? Meanwhile, there were other tempting offers coming in to go back to a corporate chief human resource officer role with significant financial benefits or be the HR head for an even bigger development organization. She could save even more of the world. Yet, now it was time to apply her purpose to herself. Things had come to a head, and she really couldn't ignore the signal.

Again, faced with several good options that she had created, she chose the one where she could fully live her purpose, including applying it to herself. Her decisions some years ago would have been very different. She decided to take the role of director of public-private partnerships at the World Food Programme, where she works with corporations to raise money to save more lives with food and leverage their expertise to end hunger. The gift of this role is that the operational speed is different, exercising different muscles as it were, allowing some focus on herself and being the mom she wants to be, while, yes, saving the world in a different way. You can sense her new enthusiasm:

We need everyone to come together to achieve Zero Hunger. With a long track record of groundbreaking, innovative, global and local partnerships, WFP sets a high standard for meaningful private sector relationships that combine technical assistance and knowledge transfer with financial contributions not only solving global problems but also creating measurable business outcomes. For example, WFP worked with MasterCard to provide Syrian refugees in Jordan and Lebanon with food assistance via a prepaid card. Nielsen has developed a methodology for gathering data related to food insecurity via mobile phones, which has not only reduced costs but also provides more timely and accurate data on the needs of those WFP serves. UPS has optimized ground handling at airfields during emergencies, allowing food to move faster and more efficiently to those in need.

WFP has four strategic priorities for partnerships with the private sector: Emergency response and preparedness; Nutrition; Supply Chain and Retail; as well as Technology and Digital Solutions. I am keen to work with existing partners, and new ones, to amplify our collective impact in these areas, for the people we serve, and solve world hunger once and for all.

Prerana has raised money to feed more than one million people for an entire year for the WFP during 2017, as well as creating partnerships where companies can contribute their technical skills and expertise to solve complex operational issues. Prerana hasn't stopped saving the world; the difference is she is applying her purpose to herself as well. Her back pains have "miraculously" gone away. She is now living her purpose with her kids and husband in a way that she could not do for the last four years. She is around more often to hang out with them and with herself. She is practicing what it means to apply her purpose to herself. It's definitely a new chapter for her.

We can all relate to a job that takes over our lives. It's hard for our loved ones and colleagues to watch from the outside when taking care of the world and taking care of ourselves get out of balance. Like Prerana, those of us who are really driven usually must hit the wall before we stop. Applying our purpose to ourselves is the last thing we think about. I see it over and over: purpose uses our physical well-being to force us to stop and listen. And I speak from personal experience, as I have been humbled by what it really takes to apply my purpose to myself.

Take my story as a warning; this is what it looks like when you don't apply purpose to the person who most needs it: you. Remember, my purpose is "To wake you up and have you finally be home." It is so easy to apply my purpose to everyone around me. I have talked to someone for 30 minutes and in that short time helped them connect to their purpose. If you are flying out for a job interview, sit next to me on the flight; you will get the job after talking to me while airborne. My purpose is about helping others access and know their unique gift. I really can bring people "home."

So, how do I bring this purpose to myself? Here is the story of a time when I didn't, and what happened. At the time—about 20 years ago—I didn't have any idea about the language of my purpose statement, yet I was living my purpose just as you have been living yours all the time. Remember, purpose is always working through us; the opportunity is to be more conscious of it.

In my early thirties I received my master's degree in organizational development and left my career in engineering. I truly enjoyed my newfound profession. I got to help launch a set of large and extremely successful change efforts. I ended up calling the authors of two books I valued highly to let them know what I had done and get their advice. I ended up going to work for one of them and quickly stepped into a fast-paced world of results-driven change efforts. Was I saving the world? Not per se, but I was focused on applying my gifts to everyone I met. And I had the gift of selling as well as the gift of doing the work—put me on a plane and by the time the flight was done, the person next to me was signing me up to work with him or her. This did wonders for my ego and I became very, very busy. Was I living my purpose? Absolutely. But since I didn't really know what my purpose was, my only access point was through applying it to others. If you needed to get tangible business results in 30, 60, or 90 days, I was your guy. Do it for thousands of people? No problem. I was working with the crew that created the GE workout process and the sky was the limit.

This high-octane life included weekly business-class flights to Munich at times as well as to every part of the United States. Yet, something wasn't 100 percent right, as five years into this crazy adventure my body began to push back. Instead of resting overnight and waking up on top of the world, it was taking me three or four days to recover from those flights. Things became worse and soon it took almost a week before I felt "normal." When you are running that fast and having such a positive impact on those you are serving, you ignore these things. At least I did.

I hit the trip wire when I was running a one-year program on change and leadership that suddenly ended at month six. The politics was complicated, and I was let go not because of bad performance but rather because I was producing results that were too positive. How is this possible? The program had received such good press that another internal group decided to take charge of it. To do that, they needed to move aside those of us they saw as a threat to their future success.

The minute I wasn't taking care of everyone else and getting all the positive energy and feedback, I crashed. I ended up basically sleeping for three months. The doctors poked and prodded me every which way to figure out what was going on. My adrenals were shot, my digestive system was not working at all, and I was hypoglycemic and didn't know it.

When things start to go wrong, everything seems to fall apart all at once. The consulting firm I worked for asked me to leave. My wife no longer wanted to be married to me; we divorced. To say nothing was going my way was an understatement. I was the poster child for what happens when you focus on saving everyone else and don't take care of yourself.

Over time I slowly regained my energy. When so many bad things happen at the same time, it's helpful to find something that recharges you. The only thing that truly felt satisfying at my core, that brought me "home," was sailing. At first, I just happened to have a friend who took me out one day. I noticed that something changed as the wind, sun, and water allowed my mind to go quiet. That August I took a sailing course, at the time a real stretch physically, yet the most satisfying thing I had done in years.

In the fall I had one of the best days of my life. It was an early October weekday and the temperature in Boston Harbor was in the 70s. I took out a small sailboat and was the only one out. The most perfect fall day and the harbor was all mine. I took it as a huge message that I was worth it.

I believe the biggest challenge most of us have, and the reason we don't apply our purpose to ourselves, is we don't think we are worthy of it. Everyone else deserves what we give them. But can we see that we too are worthy? For me, and many of the people I have worked with, it takes a crucible experience or at a minimum remembering one that almost took us out. I am astonished by how often a physical condition is part of the message. For Prerana it was her back and for me it was my gut.

Does it require a crucible experience like mine to get the message? No. The good news is, many of those who have clarified their purpose have been able to quickly identify the one or two things that really bring them joy and satisfaction and put them front and center as part of their life. They have come to understand, through either experience or luck, the importance of saving themselves first.

The activities they pursue range from something as simple as setting up a weekly date night to taking dancing classes, playing soccer in an adult league, swimming, running, writing short stories, painting, cycling, storytelling, being in nature, photography, cooking, boxing, horseback riding, skiing, reading biographies, coaching kids' volleyball, mountain climbing, singing opera, playing piano, fixing cars. Each of us has something that, when we do it, we lose ourselves and feel as if we are getting a direct hit of oxygen. One challenge is that we should have access to it regularly.

We started this chapter asking, "Do you have to save the world to live your purpose?" By now you see that saving the world is for most of us the most comfortable means of experiencing our purpose. It's a compelling experience to be in direct contact with someone who benefits from the unique gift that we bring. In some ways, the challenge is that we get addicted to these moments and allow ourselves to put the one person who most needs oxygen—ourselves—to the side.

You, me, all of us are worthy of being the recipient of our unique gift to the world, our purpose. How we bring this gift of ours to the organizations we lead in is the focus of our next chapter.

Points to ponder

1. How do you impact the world around you in your work and your life?
2. What moments bring you the most meaning in your daily job?
3. When do you experience positively impacting someone directly and get to see the results?
4. Think of when someone else did something for you that was really meaningful. Was it when you were doing really well or when you felt the most vulnerable and challenged?
5. What is the one thing that gives you oxygen that you are not doing enough of, or not frequently enough, that it's time to get back to?

Chapter 15

IMPACT: ORGANIZATIONAL PURPOSE—WHAT REALLY WORKS?

When you're surrounded by people who share a passionate commitment around a common purpose, anything is possible...

—Howard Schultz, in an interview with *Forbes*

We have talked a great deal about the impact of purpose on how we lead. What we have not talked about until now is purpose's impact on organizations. Most of us work in organizations, and the importance of the alignment between our own purpose and the purpose leading our organization can't be overstated. This alignment happens in two ways: when our purpose becomes the organization's purpose, and when we find the alignment between our purpose and the organization's. We will review both these scenarios.

Organizations as expressions of the founder's purpose

It's hard to think about Southwest Airlines without thinking of its iconic founder, Herb Kelleher. In the same way, we can't separate Teach for America from Wendy Kopp, Apple from Steve

Jobs, or Tata Industries from Jamshedji Tata. In each case, it is clear that the organization's purpose emerged from the founder's. However, less apparent are the sacrifices, self-examination, and hundreds—often thousands—of "hard rights" it took to sustain the alignment between the founder's individual purpose and that of the organization.

Few stories show this more clearly than that of Starbucks founder Howard Schultz. The story of Starbucks is a dynamic journey through having purpose, losing it, and getting it back. This rare chance to see all these elements within the narrative of one organization and a single individual allows us to clearly appreciate the gift that purpose can be when it affects an organization.

In 1982, looking to make his mark in the business world, freshly minted MBA Howard Schultz took a job as head of marketing for a small coffee company in Seattle. It didn't take long for him to fall in love with coffee, but it wasn't until a year later, while on a business trip to Milan, that he stepped into a small coffee bar and his whole world changed:

> People think I'm the founder of Starbucks. I was an employee when Starbucks only had four stores. I was sent to Italy on a trip for Starbucks and came back with this feeling that the business Starbucks was in was the wrong business. What I wanted to bring back was the daily ritual and the sense of community and the idea that we could build this third place between home and work in America. It was an epiphany. I was out of my mind. I walked in and saw this symphony of activity, and the

romance and the theater of coffee. And coffee being at the center of conversation, creating a sense of community. That is what spoke to me.

When I first heard this story, I knew I was being given a view into Howard Schultz's purpose. He isn't the first stranger to walk into a coffee bar in Italy, but the unique lens through which he looked at the world allowed him to see something that others had not: the possibility for a coffee bar to create a sense of connection and community at a scale no one had ever considered.

I believe that what became the core essence of Starbucks's purpose, *To inspire and nurture the human spirit*, is Howard Schultz's purpose as well. Selling a cup of coffee was a means, not an end in itself. He saw the possibility of creating a connection with each customer; the beautiful theater of making exquisite espresso was a means by which he could fulfill "inspiring and nurturing the human spirit."

By the late 1990s, the growing reach of this alignment of purpose was impossible to ignore. People who had never tasted a latte or a cappuccino now swore by their personalized experience and the friendly baristas who crafted it. In less than two decades Starbucks had gone from a relatively unheard-of Seattle coffee chain of less than two dozen stores to a multinational, multimillion-dollar organization with thousands of locations.

Starbucks had revolutionized not only the kinds of coffee beverages Americans were drinking and where they were enjoying them, but also *how* that coffee was getting to them and *who* was making it. Looking at the world through the unique lens of inspiring and nurturing the human spirit has many interesting outcomes. Starbucks pioneered fair sourcing efforts to ensure that farmers were treated well and paid fairly. In a world where employees usually take the hit and watch their benefits erode, Starbucks went in the opposite direction by providing employee benefits that Schultz called, coolly, "Your Special Blend." Encompassing health care, retirement benefits, college education funding, and company equity, the package went far beyond what most full-time benefit plans include, and, what's more, Schultz did the unheard-of by allowing 20-hour-a-week part-timers to participate. It's one thing to offer this in a 20-person company; Starbucks has over 200,000 employees.

Yet, the excitement and energy that Schultz felt at the onset of his journey had all but disappeared after 17 years at the helm. Knowing that his lack of engagement was a danger to the organization, he stepped down from all day-to-day duties as CEO in 2000, assuming the role of chairman and focusing on the brand's global presence.

Over the next five years, Schultz watched from the wings as Starbucks continued its meteoric rise. With growth efforts booming and annual revenue and profit increases averaging around 20 percent, a culture of rapid expansion took hold. By 2007 it became apparent to Schultz, as well as others, that Starbucks was straying from its purpose. And while "To inspire and nurture the human spirit one person, one cup, and one neighborhood at a time" might have still been painted on the walls, the organizational purpose they were living day-to-day started to feel more like "Grow! Grow! Grow!"

It's hard to imagine two more disparate statements coming from the same organization, yet this is what happens when organizations lose touch with their roots. As Schultz described it, "We had lost sight of our shared purpose and our guiding principles, in which growth and success began to cover up mistakes and a disease set into Starbucks. That disease, hubris. We lost our way...." As he watched his beloved company make decision after decision that put growth above purpose, Schultz was faced with a hard-right-versus-easy-wrong dilemma: stay safe, stay out of the way, or listen to his purpose and step back into the fray.

He knew what going back would mean, the sacrifices that would be required of him and his family and the choices he undoubtedly would have to make. But he understood something else, something that any of us who have stood in the room of purpose come to understand: that, in the end, our purpose leads us to take action.

In January 2008, Howard Schultz once again assumed the role of CEO. The move was risky. Shareholders had been getting increasingly antsy over the stalled growth margins Starbucks had been putting up, and any changes he made would be heavily scrutinized.

The transition was not an easy one. The economy was in a free fall the likes of which had not been seen since the Great Depression. Schultz was forced to make a series of critical decisions. People would feel the impact; there was no way around it. Schultz closed 600 underperforming stores.

Perhaps the purest expression of his personal purpose becoming one with the organization's came when he encountered a problem that irked him to his very core and went against everything Starbucks had been founded on: Baristas all over the country no longer knew how to pour espresso. The magical moment in the coffee shop in Italy, the one that had opened his eyes to his future, was at risk. Employee turnover rates had soared, managers didn't have the time or resources to properly train new hires, and the beverages were paying the price. The quality of the coffee "experience," the one thing that Starbucks had clung to even in its darkest hours, was no longer a given. For Schultz, that simply could not stand.

With Wall Street breathing down his neck, stock prices plummeting, and thousands of employees to retrain, Schultz made the only decision his purpose would allow. In February 2008 he closed every single Starbucks in the United States—7,100 shops—and taught 135,000 baristas how to pour the perfect shot. The move was unprecedented and cost Starbucks millions. What CEO in his or her right mind closes stores to retrain employees while already operating on a razor-thin margin?

As Schultz tells it, "All I had was my belief that, even more than perfecting our coffee, we had to restore the passion and the commitment that everyone at Starbucks needed to have for our customers. Doing so meant taking a step back before we could take many steps forward."

Remember: Purpose, the unique gift we bring to the world, serves as a set of glasses through which we see the world. When we align our purpose with our organization's, we are inviting everyone else to share our unique vision—to give our lens prescription a try, as it were. As we see in Howard Schultz's journey, this is not a task to be taken lightly, and not something that is easy to do by any means. However, when done successfully, when individual and organizational purpose operate as one, it is a rare and beautiful occurrence that can make a difference and maybe even change the world.

Why does organizational purpose matter?

Beyond the Starbucks story, organizational purpose has received a lot of hype in the last couple of years. Everyone has grabbed onto the totem of organizational purpose, and for good reason. Studies have shown that stock values of purpose-driven organizations outperform others within the same space from 133 percent to 386 percent. And these insights are not new. In 1994, the research of James Collins and Jerry Porras looked back to 1926 and found that purpose-driven companies had performed 15 times better than the overall stock market since that time.

If this isn't really news, why is organizational purpose such a big topic today? The main reason is that the pillar of strategic planning that many of us have stood on for most of the twentieth and early twenty-first centuries is now very fragile. Who has a "strategic plan" that lasts longer than the yearly budget cycle? The VUCA world impacts every industry. Strategy has been truncated to quarterly tactics, and the tactical has become a weekly sprint communicated via mobile apps.

Remember, as we look at the journey we have been on with purpose, we have learned that purpose

- Serves as a unique lens that lets us see opportunities others can't see.
- Allows us to make decisions in situations full of ambiguity.

- Supports us in choosing the hard right versus the easy wrong.
- Is the one thing that doesn't change with time or circumstances.

Organizational purpose is like your own individual purpose: it doesn't change. It's the one constant. Everything else changes all the time, so it is critical that the two things that don't—your individual and organizational purposes—are clearly understood and connected.

To discover your organization's purpose, look for that which has always been present in the organization, the thing that has always defined it and that it can do best. Just as you looked to magical moments from your own childhood, look now to the founding years and key experiences that created the organization. The crucible moments are just that—every organization has had them. In the same way, every organization is passionate about something.

If the organization you are a part of has a purpose, then you can trace it back to the beginning of the organization. Notice how the purpose showed up time after time over the years. What happened when the organization acted in alignment with its purpose? What happened when it didn't? See the pattern and the resilience of the purpose. This process is a great way to test your hypothesis about an organization's purpose to see if it really is "the one."

When you multiply the impact you have seen in this book by everyone in the organization, you start to get a sense of what is possible when you unleash purpose. An organization's purpose drives strategic choices. A Deloitte study demonstrated that purpose-driven organizations have a unique investment pattern:

- New tech (38% vs. 19% at organizations without a clear purpose)
- New markets (31% vs. 21%)
- New products and services (27% vs. 17%)
- Employee development and training (25% vs. 11%)

In short, purpose-driven organizations are willing to be more aggressive with their strategic bets than other organizations are.

How do you make organizational purpose work?

But who is doing all these incredible things, making these daring and innovative investments? It's not the invisible, faceless organization. It comes down to people like you and me living our own purpose on the stage of an organization's compelling purpose. When you divorce individual purpose from organizational purpose, you may end up with a great slide deck or presentation, but what happens a month from now? When a leader can talk about his or her own purpose and how it is connected to the organization's purpose, *that* is powerful.

In fact, organizational purpose can be so powerful that many companies hire a consulting firm, ad agency, or marketing firm with the sole desired outcome of creating the organization's purpose. Just as you shouldn't pick a string of high-minded or sugar-coated words that will please HR and imagine you have found your own personal purpose, nobody can just instill a compelling purpose in an organization and expect it to stick. Remember, purpose is what allows us to create meaning in our lives, in our organization, and for ourselves. Here is the challenge. Who really creates meaning for you? In truth, each of us creates our own meaning. Others can offer a filter, but only we can actually discover the meaning for ourselves. Thus, if you don't know your own purpose and the organization defines its purpose from the outside in…yes, you can "get behind" it—but can you be fully in the game?

Over the last 10 years of working with leaders in the area of purpose, I have seen a lot of things that have worked and many that haven't. There are some nonnegotiable characteristics of every successful attempt to instill purpose and meaning in an organization:

1. You can't fake it.
2. It matters who gets the key roles in the organization.
3. How you run meetings must be an expression of the purpose.
4. Get out of the way when the troops get it.

You can't fake it

If you have been paying attention at all, by now you have realized that purpose isn't something you can make up or fake. In good times, it may be possible to just buy into an organization's purpose and act congruently. We all have gone to great meetings and events with the jugglers, slick videos, beautiful locations, and fireworks. But when things are not going well, everyone notices if the leaders really have embodied the organization's purpose. If you don't know the purpose that is leading you, how can you fully commit to it? One of the greatest gifts of knowing and leading from purpose is the ability to step up and lead in the hard times.

Let's return to Howard Schultz and Starbucks at exactly that dark moment in summer 2008. How do you lead from a purpose such as to inspire and nurture the human spirit when you are smack in the middle of the worst-case scenario? You have closed 600 stores and eliminated 1,000 nonstore positions, the stock is worth less than half what it was a year before, and for the first time you report a net quarterly loss of $6.7 million.

On top of this you are getting suggestions to sell the company, and investors want you to undo your company-owned-and-operated store model and franchise the system, with shops just paying Starbucks a royalty. Others are suggesting reducing the quality of the roast by 5 percent—no one will notice. Lots of people are telling you the most obvious way to save $30 million is to cancel the biennial meeting of 10,000 partners.

Most of us remember 2008. What did your leaders do during that period? I personally watched almost every corporate event be canceled or "delayed."

Howard Schultz didn't franchise, compromise on the quality, or cancel the gathering of 10,000 partners. His purpose helped him see that while cutting costs might help them stay afloat for a while longer, if they didn't invest in their people, Starbucks would not survive. As Schultz often says, "Coffee is what we sell as a product, but it's not the business we're in. We're in the people business."

This takes me back to that coffee shop in Italy and his *aha!* moment about the human connection of the barista serving him espresso. Purpose doesn't care about what others think, it makes us act with real impact in the challenging times.

Schultz also decided to publicly announce Starbucks Shared Planet at this crazy moment. Shared Planet included more farmer support centers in East Africa, ethically sourcing 100 percent of Starbucks coffee by 2015 and doubling their purchase of fair-traded coffee in 2009, affecting thousands of farmers.

How many of us would have done this if our business was in such dire straits?

In hindsight it all looks brilliant, as today Starbucks's stock is worth 20 times what it was at its lowest. But in that moment, it seems Howard Schultz was listening and leading from purpose.

You can't fake leading from your purpose, especially when things are really challenging. I know you are probably thinking, "Well, what can I do? I am not the founder of my own organization." Finding the link between the organization's purpose and our own is like that moment in the coffee shop in Italy. It hits you and you don't forget it. It's not an intellectual process, but one that touches the heart and soul. When we lead from that part of ourselves we can face anything.

It matters who gets key roles in the organization

It should come as no surprise that a huge factor in the success or failure of organizational purpose is who gets picked for key roles. Those of us who are authentic and purpose-driven easily identify the ones who are just playing the system. When you bring purpose into focus within an organization, everyone gets it. They also can sense when someone isn't aligned with the organization's purpose.

Some years ago, I was running one of our programs for a very well-known purpose-led organization. By year three, each group of 30 leaders coming into our session was more energized and jazzed than the one before. The combination of what was happening outside the classroom with what we were able to do in the classroom was compelling. Then it happened. The day before I was to teach the next group of 30 senior leaders, top executives sent out a major announcement of two new promotions to the C-suite. It was as if they had decided to put Darth Vader on the top team. This usually engaging and dynamic group of believers was suddenly angry and resistant. The organization picked one person that the whole system saw as fake and not aligned with the organization's purpose, and all the good things the executives had done over the last three years were erased in a moment. It took more than 18 months of hard work by the senior management team, as well as a couple of changes, to get the system back to where it had been when that promotion happened.

There are so many things we don't have control over. The one thing that is within your control is who works for you and how much they are an expression of the organization's purpose. If your organization's purpose is to "Bring energy to life," make sure you pick people who do that. If you pick someone who sucks energy from all living things you will have a huge problem on your hands!

Nothing is more visible, important, and hard to do right—so do it right.

*How you run meetings must be an expression
of the organization's purpose*

We spend a big part of our lives in these things called meetings. Organizations that successfully engage in making purpose real bring it into how they run their meetings. This insight came to me after running a session for the top team at the Development Bank of Singapore (DBS Bank). We had spent time working on their individual purposes, and we now turned to the task of rediscovering the organizational purpose.

Members of the team who had grown up in Singapore began to share stories of being children and the joy of going to the bank. One had fond memories taking her piggy bank to her aunt who was the bank teller. Others in the group talked about customer thank-you letters that had the word "joy" in them. Over time we ended up reconnecting to the organizational purpose statement of "Making banking joyful." As we tried on the glasses of "Making banking joyful," we started to find a great number of examples of where the bank really had done exactly that over the years.

By the end of the discussion, the group had gone from literally expelling the person who had suggested that banking and joy were related to owning "Making banking joyful" as DBS Bank's purpose. The group felt they had reconnected to a core element of what had always been a central part of the bank. Just as each of us reconnects to the individual purpose that has always been leading through us, the same is true for organizations.

The energy that came out of that meeting—a combination of each leader "getting" their purpose as well as really reconnecting to the organization's purpose—was significant. A wide range of actions resulted that had dramatic impacts on the bank's ability to live the purpose. And, surprisingly, one I never would have thought of had one of the biggest impacts. Employees in the bank (not the top team) decided to establish a ritual of appointing a "JO" (Joyful Observer) who tracks the meeting to make sure that we are observing joyfulness in the process. This became the norm in the bank and has probably had a bigger impact on making the purpose a reality than any other single thing.

So, what would happen if you applied *your* organizational purpose to your next meeting?

Get out of the way when the troops get it

As a leader in an organization that has purpose, you will be tested. At some point, the people working for you will buy into the organization's purpose. Yet, they will need to test you to see if you really are an expression of the purpose.

When you are being tested, probably neither you nor the people testing you will realize in the moment what is going on. Purpose is like that sometimes; it's only when we look back that we actually see its hand in things. But over the years I have seen many interesting examples of the test being given. As the DBS Bank organization began to realize that CEO Piyush Gupta and the top team were serious about living "Making banking joyful," many great things occurred beyond the meeting mantra. In the short span of one year, an impressive number of initiatives and projects connected to the purpose emerged:

1. We embraced "journey thinking," taught this to all our leadership, and ran over 400 customer and employee journeys over two years. The journeys were focused on saving customer hours and creating a truly joyful experience.
2. We committed resources to the process, including technology prioritization and physical space. We remodeled our work spaces in a program called "Joyspace" and set aside rooms for journey teams to work in.
3. We changed our Balanced Scorecard to introduce a set of "Making Banking Joyful (MBJ)" KPIs so we could measure our progress. This constitutes 20 percent of the scorecard.
4. We modified our external marketing to capture the MBJ experience.

More importantly from an adoption perspective, the purpose has become the way that everyone in the bank looks at every process. Each DBS Bank employee from the top level all the way down asks at every step, "Did XYZ really 'make banking joyful'?"

Forbes even featured CEO Piyush Gupta in an article titled "Can DBS Bank Make Banking Joyful?" that describes the impact.

All of these things and more is what we all want to see happen. Yet, along came the test. Every year, DBS Bank faces a situation that captures the benefit of its purpose as well as a key challenge it faces: In the two weeks prior to Chinese New Year, the tradition in Singapore is to turn all the old money in for new money. You can imagine the impact of everyone changing money on wait time at a retail bank. Someone deep inside DBS Bank decided to put portable ATMs at the busiest locations in Singapore for those two weeks. The CEO was complimented during a TV interview for saving everyone time waiting in line, giving him the chance to say, "We make banking joyful." After the interview, he got on the phone with his CIO and asked, "Who did this and why wasn't I involved in the decision?" The CIO responded, "Well, if we are going to make banking joyful, we need to get you out of being involved in every decision!"

Purpose will test us to find the deeper wisdom and ability to allow others the autonomy, mastery, and purpose that are theirs to fulfill. Sometimes we need help from our colleagues to pass the test.

Let's return to Jostein Solheim's adventure at Ben & Jerry's (chapter 1). Jostein Solheim's purpose statement is "Helping people thrive in paradox and ambiguity for things that *really* matter." Clearly, he is not Ben or Jerry, and his Norwegian accent will remind you that he didn't grow up in Vermont.

He was working with employees who had been there when Ben and Jerry were running the show, who knew what living the firm's purpose felt and looked like. Jostein had made great strides over the previous 18 months. Yet, there must always be a test.

Jostein's test came when the head of product development proposed they release the flavor called Schweddy Balls. When the head of product development proposed launching a new ice cream based on the infamous *Saturday Night Live* skit starring Alec Baldwin, at first Jostein rejected it out of hand. Then he said yes.

Corporate America hated the flavor; consumers couldn't get enough. Walmart's CEO asked his team not to sell Schweddy Balls, which should give us all a moment of pause. Schweddy Balls became a huge marketing success for Ben & Jerry's. Every news outlet had to talk about it. Nobody in the 2011 Christmas season escaped without wondering what it would taste like. Ben & Jerry's was back to being the crazy brand that does what others won't do and can't get away with.

So why did he do it, really? Launching one flavor that was slightly inappropriate could have snowballed, resulting in all Ben & Jerry's flavors being pulled from shelves, negative publicity, upset customers, and more. And some of that did happen: an influential mothers' group was very unhappy to hear their kids talking about "Schweddy Balls." Some major retailers were displeased, and it took a while to build back the trust needed to grow the business over time. Yet Jostein knew it was the test he had to pass to demonstrate to the employees that he was committed to what Ben & Jerry's stood for. Would he step up and show that he could really live the organization's mission and purpose? Would he cave to his bosses and to the major retailers and say, No, we really are not going to be Ben & Jerry's, or was he going to demonstrate, by doing something that was a beautiful example of this crazy, wonderful, slightly inappropriate iconic brand, that his individual and organizational purposes were aligned?

After that moment, the employees all realized that Jostein was fully in the game. The key people who are the soul of Ben & Jerry's have become Jostein's greatest supporters. Recently, Ben told Jostein that he has "out-Ben'd" him. That congruency and alignment have allowed Ben & Jerry's, one of the first premium ice creams, to go from single-digit declining numbers in Jostein's early days to double-digit growth today. Jostein will tell you, "I didn't do any of the things that made it happen," and, in some ways, he is right. Yet, if he hadn't passed the Schweddy Balls test, I don't think the key people would have stayed around or that the magic would have grown to what it is today.

Organizations don't pass tests; we do. Not all of us get the chance—as Alec Baldwin, the *SNL* team, and the crew at Ben & Jerry's did—to make us smile a little more than we would have otherwise. And yet we each have a purpose that, if we step fully into allowing it to lead us, will matter not just to us but to our organization as well. The alignment between who we are and the organization is the difference that makes the difference. You can run your meetings and promote people just like everyone else— but in doing so, don't expect results that are any different from anyone else's. Or you can listen to the purpose that is leading the organization, along with the purpose that is leading you, and never look back.

Chapter 16

MASTERY IN THE ROOM OF PURPOSE

> It is not the critic who counts; not the man who points
> out how the strong man stumbles, or where the doer of
> deeds could have done them better. The credit belongs
> to the man who is actually in the arena, whose face
> is marred by dust and sweat and blood; who strives
> valiantly;
>   ...who at the worst, if he fails, at least fails while
> daring greatly, so that his place shall never be with those
> cold and timid souls who neither know victory nor defeat.
>   —Theodore Roosevelt

With her foreword to this book, Brené Brown started us on our journey to examine the impact of leading from purpose. I would like to end our time together with Brené's favorite speech, one that anchors her book *Daring Greatly*. Let's look at Roosevelt's text through the lens of purpose.

Are you in the arena, or are you one of those cold and timid souls who neither know victory nor defeat? It's a powerful question that captures the reality of leading from purpose. Many of us answer *yes*, we want to be in the arena. Yet, for those of us— including myself—whose stories you have read in these pages, the fact is that our purpose is always in the arena. The challenge is to fully listen. Mastery of leading from purpose is a journey; over time, we step in and we step out of the arena. When I first read Roosevelt's words, I immediately understood that his "arena" is the room of purpose that we have been referencing throughout the book.

Each chapter in part III, starting with chapter 6's dive into clarity and confidence, touches on a different way we experience leading from purpose. The chapters share examples of people who were actually "in the arena," including Everett, who was a first responder at the Boston Marathon bombing, and Jacqui, whose actions turned around a hardware retailer; and ending with Jostein's continuing saga from the previous chapter. When everyone else is waiting on the sidelines, with purpose we become the one who takes action. Leading isn't about telling everyone else what to do; it is about taking steps that, over time, others wish to follow.

Purpose leads you where you need to go

Purpose is a sharp sword. Once you know what your purpose is, you also know immediately when you are leading from it and when you are not. The moment you find your purpose is a moment of waking up; once awake, you see. You instantly stand in the room of purpose (Roosevelt's arena). You know what is at stake and you have a level of motivation and commitment that transcends that of the cold and timid souls sitting on the sidelines.

When I ask leaders to look back at the last six months and identify those moments, actions, or events that were purposeful and the ones that were not, they find it easy to create the lists. There can be no mastery without discernment. One of the gifts of purpose is the ability to move toward personal transformation and real mastery, stepping fully into the room of purpose that you are meant to be in.

Dolf—whose compelling Congo experience we shared earlier—is one of those executives who has always been on the fast track. Dolf's purpose is *"Be the gardener with boundless curious energy to grow a better world."* Dolf and I have often talked about his powerful experiences as he lives his purpose. Still, the most transparent, poignant, and helpful discussion we ever had was one that focused on the times when he *wasn't* a powerful expression of his purpose.

Dolf was given a gift. His brain processes information and figures out the answer faster than most of us. This has significant upsides and huge downsides. If your purpose is to be the gardener, you must give people room to grow. Dolf does that in remarkable ways. You will not find a better use of his gift than when he gives presentations to his organization, or sits down for supportive one-on-ones to tackle difficult issues, or synthesizes complicated data to find the answer that benefits everyone.

His challenge has been using that smart brain in his management team meetings. His purpose has taken him to task in a way that no person ever could. He has realized that he can appear too pushy, too involved in the content, and too quick to solve complex problems while leaving his team behind. A couple of years ago, he learned this by hiring a coach to interview his team to help him improve his game. The 360-degree feedback report showed the great downside of not living his purpose with his team. He had to help people grow by letting them think and figure things out on their own, and not do it all himself.

This has probably been his toughest lesson as a leader, and he has come a long way since that time. Many of us can relate to Dolf's dilemma—being asked to choose between being in service to his purpose as opposed to satisfying his urge to be the smartest person in the room. Following our purpose instead of staying in our place of comfort creates an interesting tension. It takes maturity and wisdom to enter the room, step into the arena, away from the comfort of the stands. We have all been told, repeatedly, to focus on our strengths and leverage them, but what happens when they get in the way of our purpose? Dolf learned that solving all the problems all the time didn't solve anything or grow anyone. Instead, it kept the team weak and dependent on him. The team knew they didn't have to show up—Dolf would do it anyway.

When Dolf received his feedback report from the coach, his initial reaction was the same one any of us would have had: he looked for reasons not to believe the data or to justify it. Dolf could have easily ignored the feedback and continued overleveraging his ability to solve everyone's problems all the time. Standing in the room of purpose was his wise move at that moment. He could be the "smartest person in the room" for the rest of his life and let go of his purpose in a leadership role, or he could fulfill his purpose. Clearly, his rapid mental processing is an essential capability in many other contexts and situations...just not with the team.

This story contains a great set of insights as to what real

mastery looks like. Purpose allows us to see that we have to choose how we show up and what our impact will be on others. Much of the narrative out there these days is "Focus on what you are good at." Purpose will tell us, "You want true mastery? Then let's get in the arena. Step back in the room of purpose and let's work toward the real impact your unique life was meant to bring."

Leaving our comfort zone will be awkward at first. Luckily, we'll find that feeling of flow and ease again once we master that next level of leading from our purpose. Dolf has become more at peace with letting his team struggle and discover the answer, instead of giving in to the urge to solve the problem himself. It's not his natural tendency—and probably never will be—so he has to make the choice every time. He has learned that what feels good in the moment isn't what is satisfying over time when our purpose is keeping score.

How do we step back into the room of purpose?

It's not like anyone has ever spent their life 100 percent living their purpose, but when you know your purpose, you have a choice. Do you step into the room or not? I have found that the process follows a cycle, as noted in the graphic on page 252.

It would be nice to think that we never fall off track. Instead, over time, we shorten the cycle time. The opportunity is to welcome the cycle as the ultimate gift of purpose. A colleague once told me a story about the creator of aikido, who was asked by the emperor to teach the other martial arts teachers his form. After several lessons, the other masters became despondent because

the aikido master never was caught off balance. His response was that he was *always* off balance and in a continuous state of rebalancing. Purpose works the same way.

How do we discover the deeper truth? In the best case, we realize that we are not leading from purpose in a given moment, reflect on how we would bring our purpose to this situation, then step back into the room of purpose and lead. Yes, for many of us, it is actually that simple and it really works. I am always surprised at the effect this simple act can have on how I feel and what I actually say or do.

In other cases, the reminder that we should step into the room of purpose comes from someone else. In Chapter 9: "Standing on Solid Ground," where I focus on identity, we saw how powerful it is when someone speaks to our purpose. Most of us remember vividly when others have called us into the arena! Here's an example from my own journey.

I teach programs on purpose regularly. During one program, I felt off my game. The audience contained some highly cynical participants, including one who looked and acted like an old mentor. Usually I can deal with cynical participants with great aplomb, but on this day the combination of cynicism and the reminder of a challenging mentor got the better of me. I didn't feel like I was in my room of purpose, but rather in a deep pit—and I was dragging the participants in with me. That evening I sat down with the head of talent and development for the company and let her know that I was off my game and struggling. She looked me in the eye and said, "So, where is the Nick that I know and have seen? How can I help him show up right now?" In that moment, I felt she was talking to my purpose and inviting me back into the room. It wasn't what she said, but rather the direct invitation to step back into the room of purpose. It was an energizing and validating moment of deeper truth, as if I had awakened from deep sleep. The good news is that the deeper truth most of us need to be reminded of is the unique gift we bring to the world, our purpose. The next day was a very different experience for the participants and for myself. I engaged with the mentor double about his impact and we ended up having a good laugh as he recalled when he had once found himself in a similar situation.

Let's return to Dolf's journey to reach his purpose-led behavior of talking less in meetings. It was the opposite of what he was comfortable doing, yet it was what his purpose was asking him to do. After that realization, Dolf put a mechanism in place to hear the deeper truth.

Reviewing his 360-degree report with his team, Dolf discussed the shift he needed to make and the feedback he wanted, identifying a couple of people to give him feedback after each meeting. He chose management team members who are not his direct reports, because, as you can imagine, asking a direct report for feedback is challenging at best. The key is to find someone we truly trust, who's neutral enough to tell us the deeper truth. Another challenge is to pick someone who will keep the discussion confidential. Stacey, whom we met in the chapter on crucible stories, was one of Dolf's feedback resources. As head of communications assigned to Dolf's team, she reported to a corporate boss. Stacey's purpose statement is "To ignite the worthy fight and blow your hair back," so I really wish I could be a fly on the wall when she gives immediate feedback. Dolf had the courage to pick people with nothing at stake who cared deeply about his success.

Sometimes we don't have a trusted person to remind us; instead, the universe just whacks us on the head. My personal example of receiving deeper truth in this way is not as much fun as my first story, but it is a very effective demonstration of the power of stepping back into the room of purpose.

Recently, I ran a program that I felt scored a 10 out of 10. Over a three-day period I successfully brought that wonderful combination of insight and humor to a group of executives. There was only one problem: the participants didn't think it went well at all. Their English language skills were okay, but not excellent. The program feedback was consistent: I talked way too fast and they felt I was laughing at them instead of with them. If my purpose is to wake you up and have you be home, I really screwed up. Turns out my humor didn't translate well; I had allowed my desire to hear myself say interesting things and be entertaining to take the place of leading from my purpose. As I look back on that program, when I spoke with some of the participants during the breaks it had been obvious that understanding English required real effort on their part. I had wondered why everyone was checking their phones during the program. Later I learned that they were looking up words in an effort to understand what I was saying. Since that day, I now seek out the participant with the least English skills to be my advisor. I ask that person to raise his or her hand when I talk too fast or use obscure U.S.-centric references or words that sound great to me and mean absolutely nothing to them.

Purpose is a continuous journey of discovering a deeper truth that brings us to a fuller understanding of our unique gift.

Going deeper into the room of purpose

Most of us have parts of our life where leading from our purpose is easier than others. Most senior executives have spent a lifetime refining their craft and how they bring it to the world. For myself and many of the leaders I have worked with, the workplace has been this domain. Sure, we can always improve our leadership at the office, but the big step up in leading from purpose is in a different arena.

This is the question I ask: *Where would living your purpose as a leader more fully bring you the most joy and satisfaction?* For those still striving to make it to the top of their profession, the answer frequently is making a key decision or changing the strategy of a business. Yet the most successful leaders respond, "family and personal life."

I have worked with many leaders who, every two or three years, have dragged their family to a new country, new school system, new culture, and new language. This exposes an interesting tension. We are giving 110 percent of our purpose to our work, but what is left over for the people we love and live with is a humbling predicament.

In earlier chapters, we heard from Ryan's journey with his mentally and physically handicapped daughter, as well as Prerana's challenge of saving the world and its toll on her health and family. Both these stories remind us that there are opportunities to go deeper into leading from purpose than the work challenges we face. Perhaps this is because most of our difficult moments at work have a beginning, a middle, and an end. The end, 95 percent of the time, is a success story of redemption and renewal. Think of Ranjay: He didn't get the job he thought he should, and still used his purpose to support others. And then, almost by magic, he received a big promotion. If we stay at it long enough, we come out on top of the challenge. Even in the times where things go badly and never recover, there is a next chapter in which we have the big *aha!* and learn what we need to do to put us back on top.

Yet our family and personal lives seem different. The adventure is long term for most of us or has so many layers of complexity that there is no easy solution. All our usual means of vanquishing risk by solving the underlying issue are rendered useless. We must find a deeper place within us, and over time there can be a deeper peace. Yet we can't usually take back what has happened or fix what was not done. This is where purpose can have its greatest impact. This is the arena that truly matters. I have a story to tell you to help make the point.

About four years ago, I had just come home from running a powerful program. At that time, I was a divorced single dad with daughters ages 16 and 13. (You have met Renee and Keely earlier in this book.) That weekend I was responsible for chauffeuring the girls to their many activities. My goal was to make up for all the times I wasn't around (basically 90 percent of the time, and I owe my ex-wife and her husband a deep debt of gratitude for driving the girls to every possible thing).

For the first 24 hours things went smoothly as I took them shopping and drove them to social engagements, then it all fell apart. Saturday evening I dropped off 16-year-old Renee at a party, then took Keely, the 13-year-old, to a babysitting job. I went to dinner to kill time. I picked up Keely at 10 p.m. sharp, as requested. I was supposed to pick up Renee at 11 p.m. and showed up 15 minutes early, to her great dismay. On the way home she had a meltdown because she was so embarrassed to be picked up before everyone else. All the other kids got to stay and their parents waited outside, but I, who didn't know the protocol, walked in and pulled her out of the party.

At that point, 13-year-old Keely started yelling at Renee. When these two go at it, no prisoners are taken—and in those days they fought all the time, about everything. I lost it in that moment, and yelled at both of them until there was only silence.

We all do it. The issue was that it wasn't my first time with the girls. Somehow, I had decided that I could be fully in the room of purpose at work and be an exhausted, short-tempered jerk at home with my daughters.

The next morning the girls got up and told me they didn't want to spend any time hanging out with me anymore. This was a deeper truth that I really did not want to hear. I remember sitting there realizing they had a choice. Here was a guy who helped people discover their purpose but who couldn't be the wise dad when it was most needed.

I wish I had a quick fix to this, but some things take time. The truth is, it took me two or three years to repair the damage that many years of giving everything to everyone else had wrought. When I looked at my purpose, "to wake you up and have you finally be home," it hurt. I am not sure I can express the level of loss I felt for months after this event. I ended up having to look at every part of my life and re-think what it meant to be a parent.

My first step was to create a safer place for us to talk about my impact on them over the years. I had my own list of times I wish I had been less reactive in the moment. When I asked each girl to share her top-10 list of Dad overreacting, the first big surprise was that they had different lists from mine. The deeper truth is just that—it reveals an understanding of the world that we didn't see, but that, once revealed, allows us to step back into our purpose more readily. For the first time I saw how they experienced me. I saw which actions I took that brought a deep level of safety as well as the actions that had made them feel unseen.

With the help of a gifted family counselor, we slowly began to rebuild our relationship. At point Keely showed me what it looked like when I got upset. I will never forget what that felt like. Probably the only thing that got me through this process was my purpose. I kept asking myself what would allow us to feel that we were "finally home."

After a lot of hard work, we've come through it. For the last two years I have received a letter from Keely and Renee on Father's Day thanking me for being their dad and for the work I have done to be the dad I am today. The girls continue to give me regular and constant feedback on how we are doing. The deeper truth is front and center with them. I am clear that I will never really fix what happened, yet I have the choice to always step more fully into being the best dad I can be. Purpose is always there to catch me when I fall.

We all have stories of the times we have been most challenged. Writing about this one felt very risky. Yet seeing the deeper truth and stepping more fully into the room of purpose is what makes us more alive. That is one of the gifts I have learned from this work.

You might ask if there is any impact from what I did with my daughters on how I show up at work as a leader. It turns out the cranky dad was also the cranky boss in the office. As I began stepping into the room of purpose at home, I started to see just how much the same was happening in the office. I had lots of good excuses. Being jet-lagged, stressed out about delivering a new program, 24/7 emails as I address the cadence of running a global business, phone systems that decide to stop working, etc. The deeper truth was that I, as the thought leader and author of this work, was selectively stepping into the room of purpose when it was easy, and other times not. The repair process took much less work, yet it was just as important. These days, the crew in the office who have been around for a while say I am so much nicer as a boss than I used to be. There is a lot more laughter in the office. When I start to slip, Liz, my executive assistant, walks in my office and just asks, "Are you okay?" in that "You're not okay and you need to take a time-out" way, because she cares.

We are all leading from purpose one humble day at a time. On a good day I may be one step ahead of you, but that doesn't mean I don't trip and fall, too. The key is to get up quickly and step back in to the room of purpose. The challenge, as Bob Quinn, from the University of Michigan, so eloquently describes it, is that for most of us the path to get there lies through our own hypocrisy. When seeing the gap between what we say and what we do becomes too painful, we leave the places of comfort and access that inner courage to step more fully into leading from our purpose.

> We increase integrity by constantly monitoring our lack of integrity.... We refuse to see our hypocrisy. Yet seeing our hypocrisy is the potential motor for change. There is so much pain, we are willing to close our integrity gaps. Then we exercise the courage to change. We finally leave a particular comfort zone and begin a process of transformation.
>
> —Robert Quinn

Mastery through deliberate practice

Research by Anders Ericsson reinforces the benefits of the three-step model we have been exploring in Dolf's and my stories.

Ericsson has spent his life studying what differentiates those who become true masters of their discipline and those who don't. Among his findings: Masters practice very differently from the way most people do. Accomplished musicians, athletes, and other experts all do what Ericsson calls "deliberate practice." In deliberate practice, you consciously choose to step out of your comfort zone because you want to achieve something that really matters to you that is a step beyond.

- First, you must clarify the desired behavior that is a stretch for you—Dolf's desire to change his behavior in meetings is an example, or my being fully present with my daughters.
- Then set up the environment for immediate feedback—Dolf and I both put in place mechanisms to get direct feedback. Our plans may be not as rigorous as a piano virtuoso's, but they follow the same principles.
- Repeatedly perform the same or a similar behavior or task—It's the frequent repetition of the practice, in which we get the feedback over and over again, that is important.

According to Ericsson, this way of operating is all too rare. What I appreciate about Ericsson's research and insights is that the behavior or activity necessitates real effort and challenge. The "stretch" piece is critical here. Without stretch, no deliberate practice. Notice we are not talking about leveraging our well-developed strengths and doing what comes naturally to us. Rather, it is about diligently focusing on an area where we don't have real competence and spending significant time doing it repeatedly.

The feedback must be immediate to make what is a conscious level of incompetence turn, over time, into unconscious competence (something that feels natural). Once my girls became used to giving me feedback, they would say, "Dad, chill," which to all our surprise actually worked. I would take a 15-minute break and then we were on track for what we really wanted to have happen.

Let's be clear that this type of practice is taxing and humbling, and we will continue to see the gap between our performance and our desired behavior.

If we take Ericsson's research and insights and combine them with Angela Duckworth's research on what enables "grit," we find a common theme. Motivation is the one thing that has the biggest impact on those who truly master a discipline. In all cases, people who excel at what they do had the motivation to persevere and do the tough deliberate practice long enough to become a true master. The powerful truth is that natural ability isn't what determines mastery; rather, it's grit, deliberate practice, and repetition that are the keys:

- Sustained motivation determines those who become true masters.
- Sustained motivation in the face of hardship, negative feedback, lots of feedback, and going back to do what doesn't feel comfortable are essential.

Motivation, mastery, and flow

Look at your own personal experience. When have you had that level of sustained motivation? Most leaders I have worked with—and myself—have gotten excited about a new adventure, job, craft, or direction and watched that light bulb of motivation dim and go out over time. We all have bookshelves, closets, and storage rooms full of the best-in-class stuff that was required or recommended as we pursued a new discipline or craft. Some of us have completely changed professions because our motivation has waned.

If we look at the magical moments from your childhood when you were doing what you most loved to do, or the most challenging life experiences and how you faced them and thrived instead of just surviving, as well as the core passions that have stayed with you over time, what are we really looking at? Purpose is the ultimate motivation that runs through our life.

Angela Duckworth believes this as well, based on her extensive research. *"My claim here is that, for most people, purpose is a tremendously powerful source of motivation. There may be exceptions, but the rarity of these exceptions proves the rule."*

The definition of motivation is "reason for acting or behaving in a certain way." Your purpose is your core essence and reason for acting that defines you. Purpose motivates us to bring our unique gift to the world. Itzhak Perlman and Joshua Bell are world-class violinists. Both are masters of deliberate practice. Yet in playing the same piece of music, each has his signature. What stage are you meant to play your music on, and what music will it be? That is the whisper of purpose, our deepest and most pure motivation.

You're now wondering if leading from your purpose is only helpful to motivate you to do things that are hard and difficult. No, that's not true either.

When we lead from our purpose, a good deal of the time we experience a sense of "flow." It's effortless and time flies by as we feel a sense of joy. Mihaly Csikszentmihalyi has spent his life studying people in a "flow" state. The experience is that of effortlessness and the feedback is positive. All the individuals I have interviewed have a long list of activities they experience as being an expression of their purpose and an experience of "flow." Angela Duckworth has a great saying: "Deliberate practice is for preparation, and flow is for performance." Our purpose is there in both places, kicking us to do the needed hard preparation, struggle, and effort, as well as the beautiful performance that results from the many hours of invisible effort.

Once I was teaching with Nitin Nohria, now Dean of Harvard Business School, in an executive program. I was in awe of his ability to lead the case he was teaching. It was one of the most brilliant, engaging, hypnotizing, satisfying 90 minutes I had experienced in a classroom. Afterward he told me, "If they only knew the 10,000 hours of practice it took to make it look so effortless."

Purpose will have us find the joy in the practice as well as the flow moments. Purpose is the mother of all motivations.

So, as you get more clarity on what your purpose is, smile when you notice those places that matter to you where you are struggling. Know that everyone who becomes a master started with the same lack of skills and abilities that you did; they just were motivated to keep going when others stopped. Purpose isn't stopping any time soon. It has been leading you all your life. The more you own it, the more you will see the gap and leave your comfort zone for mastery in the room of purpose.

Points to ponder

1. What do you think the real score is for you at this moment on how well you are leading from your purpose?

2. In what situations would it be helpful to more fully lead from your purpose?

   a. What would be the impact to both you and others around you if you were to fully step into the room of purpose in this situation?

   b. Who in your life can help remind you of your unique gift to the world and how you can bring it to this situation?

3. When do you most feel in a state of "flow"?

   a. Describe a specific moment.

   b. How many hours of practice did it take for you to be able to experience this state of flow?

4. Where is the next place your purpose would like you to fully step into mastery?

EPILOGUE: ARRIVING AT YOUR OWN DOOR!

The time will come
when, with elation,
you will greet yourself arriving
at your own door, in your own mirror,
and each will smile at the other's welcome,

and say, sit here. Eat.
You will love again the stranger who was your self.
Give wine. Give bread. Give back your heart
to itself, to the stranger who has loved you

all your life, whom you ignored
for another, who knows you by heart.
Take down the love letters from the bookshelf,

the photographs, the desperate notes,
peel your own image from the mirror.
Sit. Feast on your life.

—Love after Love, Derek Walcott

We have come to the end of our adventure together. Derek Walcott's poem perfectly summarizes the gift and the challenge with purpose. Purpose truly is the stranger who has loved us all our life, the one we have ignored as we have valued others' opinions more than our own.

I have spent most of my life trying to arrive. I tried to be in all the places one should be, hoping that the moment would happen when I would be "witnessed" and get a seat at the table.

For most of my career, independent of how well things went and how I felt, the question I needed an answer to was this: How did I do? Whomever I assigned authority to in those moments was god. What they said determined my reality. If they felt things went well, even though some participants of a program or project hated it, all was okay. But, if they really didn't like it, even though all the feedback was great, I would be devastated.

Over the last 10 years something began to shift. Let's be clear: The external world didn't change; in fact, it became more unpredictable and crazy-making.

What changed was that as I deepened my connection to my purpose, my relationship to everyone in authority shifted. I can remember the program in London about five years ago in which the change began. At the end of that program, something inside me was at peace. I looked at what we had done and realized I was 100 percent operating from my purpose. Independent of anyone else's assessment, professional suggestions of what could be better, or participant feedback, I knew that I had given 100 percent of my purpose. It was so satisfying to be finally, fully home.

Was this program any better than all the others? Nope. Others had been more wildly successful or magical over the years. In reality, it was an average program.

As I look back at my life, the funny thing is, that moment in London wasn't the first time it had happened. If you and I had a cup of coffee and talked, I could help you find those moments in your life that feel similar. I am not talking about a mystical experience that few people have had.

The challenge is that it's such a subtle shift when it occurs. I almost missed it, again. I remember sitting down afterward in the empty classroom with the usual leftover random papers, evaluation forms not filled out, and name tags. I began writing how it felt to be in this place of peace within myself. As I wrote, I asked the question we all wonder about when we have a powerful moment: Am I here to stay? And only now, as I write this, does it all come into focus—here, now, as I write these words. You see, I actually had forgotten about that moment in London, again. Derek Walcott just says it so much better.

> *Give back your heart*
> *to itself, to the stranger who has loved you*
> *all your life, whom you ignored*
> *for another, who knows you by heart.*

The reality is that only I could give the gift of "arriving" to myself. I am never going to get an Oscar, Tony, or Nobel Prize; be a big-time CEO; win an election; or receive any of those other external markers that define arriving. It's funny, working with people who have those things—many of them are still waiting to arrive! For many of us, it's a ball that keeps getting kicked away just as we are about to grab it.

So, how do you know? How do you know when you have arrived at your own door?

There comes a point when your purpose becomes so present in how you operate in the world that you know it and so does everyone else.

Arriving doesn't come with trumpets, rather with a deepened responsibility to honor the gift of my purpose to everyone. Sometimes I do better than others, and, yes, every day I check the score.

Your purpose has always been there and will always be there.

Throughout the book I have told you my purpose is "*To wake you up and have you finally be home.*" It's a good definition of my purpose, but let me remind you that the words are just a key. Your purpose has been and always will be the same, but over time you may change the key to access it. For me, a new set of words came in the voice of a participant who walked up to me a few years ago, smiled, and said, "I like your purpose statement, and here are some words that better capture how you have shown up for me." Since then, these are the words I use to capture the unique gift that I bring to the world, my purpose. This one really makes me smile when I say it.

NICK—I am the Gandalf that knocks on your door.
If you open it, you will know the deeper truth of who you are.

This book has been my way of knocking on your door, just as Gandalf does at the beginning of *The Lord of the Rings*. When

Frodo Baggins of the Shire opens that door, he begins a journey to the deeper truth of who he is.

So, I am knocking on your door. Your purpose will lead in ways that nothing else can.

Let's Go!

You Are Now Invited to Fill Out the Leading from Purpose Self-Assessment

Please take the Leading from Purpose Self-Assessment again, to see the impact that leading from purpose is having!

www.coreleader.com/survey

Remember to compare the scores if you took the survey earlier in the book.

You can find us at www.coreleader.com if you have any questions, comments, or want more information on our work.

NOTES

PART I

Chapter 1

Page 3: **To be nobody but yourself**...Cummings, e. e. *A Miscellany*. Argophile Press, 1958.

Page 4: **All the world's a stage**...Shakespeare, William. *As You Like It*. Edited by Susan L. Rattiner. Dover Publications, 1998.

Page 9: **Everything came into being for**...Aurelius, Marcus. *The Emperor's Handbook: A New Translation of the Meditations*. Translated by C. Scot Hicks and David V. Hicks. Scribner, 2002.

Page 9: **Harvard Business School's head of**...Montgomery, Cynthia A. *The Strategist*. Ebook ed. HarperCollins, 2012.

Page 9: **Martin Seligman, the father of**...Seligman, Martin E. P. *Flourish: A Visionary New Understanding of Happiness and Wellbeing*. Free Press, 2011.

Page 9: **Daniel Pink, in his book**...Pink, Daniel, H. *Drive: The Surprising Truth About What Motivates Us*. Riverhead Books, 2009.

Page 9: **Research on woman leaders by**...Ibarra, Herminia. *Act Like a Leader, Think Like a Leader*. Kindle edition. Harvard Business Review Press, 2015.

Page 10: **Purpose is equally important at**..."The Human Era @ Work: Findings from The Energy Project and *Harvard Business Review*." 2014. PDF.

Page 10: **Another study, by the DeVry**...Levit, A., and S. Licina. *How the Recession Shaped Millennial and Hiring Manager Attitudes about Millennials' Future Careers*. Career Advisory Board, DeVry University. 2011.

Page 11: **These studies have highlighted many**...Koizumi, M., H. Ito, Y. Kaneko, and Y. Motohashi. "Effect of Having a Sense of Purpose in Life on the Risk of Death from Cardiovascular Diseases." *Journal of Epidemiology* 18, no. 5 (2008): 191–196.

Page 13: **According to the United Nations**..."Population by Age, Sex, and Urban/Rural Residence." UN Data—A World of Information, United

Nations Statistics Division, last update: 22 May 2017. http://data.un.org/Data .aspx?d=POP&f=tableCode%3A22.

Page 13:   **India alone has almost the**...Sengupta, Somini. "The World Has a Problem: Too Many Young People." *New York Times,* 5 March 2016, https://www.nytimes.com/2016/03/06/sunday-review/the-world -has-a-problem-too-many-young-people.html.

Chapter 2

Page 18:   **Xerox's PARC Lab in Palo**...Gladwell, Malcolm. "Creation Myth: Xerox PARC Lab, Apple, and the Truth about Innovation." *New Yorker,* 16 May 2011. https://www.newyorker.com/magazine/2011/05/16/creation -myth.

Page 21:   **According to Mary Gentile in**...Gentile, Mary, C. *Giving Voice to Values.* Yale University Press, 2010.

Page 24:   **Thomas Jefferson wrote the Declaration**...Stephen E. Lucas, "Justifying America: The Declaration of Independence as a Rhetorical Document," in Thomas W. Benson, ed., *American Rhetoric: Context and Criticism.* Southern Illinois University Press, 1989.

Page 24:   **During the American Civil War**...Ellis, Joseph J. *American Creation.* Knopf Doubleday, 2007.

Chapter 3

Page 34:   **Things that I grew up**...Itzkoff, Dave. "Tim Burton, at Home in His Own Head." *New York Times,* 19 September 2012, http://www .nytimes.com/2012/09/23/movies/tim-burton-at-home-in-his-own -head.html.

Chapter 4

Page 45:   **That which does not kill**...Nietzsche, Friedrich. *Twilight of the Idols.* 1889. Penguin Classics, 1990.

Page 45:   ***In Geeks and Geezers,* authors**...Bennis, Warren G., and Robert J. Thomas. *Geeks and Geezers.* Harvard Business School Publishing, 2002.

Page 55:   **I didn't discover my purpose**...George, Bill, Nick Craig, and Scott Snook. *The Discover Your True North Fieldbook.* John Wiley & Sons, 2015.

Chapter 5

Page 58:   **Our passions, simply stated, are**...Leider, Richard J. *The Power of Purpose: Find Meaning, Live Longer, Better.* MJF Books, 2000.

Page 60:   Like the narrator in Robert...Frost, Robert. *The Poetry of Robert Frost*. Edited by Edward Connery Lathem. Henry Holt & Company, 1969.

PART II

Page 69:   There's a thread you follow...William Stafford, "The Way It Is," from *Ask Me: 100 Essential Poems*. Copyright ©1998, 2014 by William Stafford and the Estate of William Stafford. Reprinted with the permission of The Permissions Company, Inc., on behalf of Graywolf Press, www.graywolfpress.org.

PART III

Chapter 6

Page 89:   The quality of being certain..."Clarity." *Oxford Dictionary of English*, 3rd ed. Oxford University Press, 2010.

Page 92:   Adapt to the prevailing level..."Focus." *Oxford Dictionary of English*, 3rd ed. Oxford University Press, 2010.

Page 93:   Faith or belief that one..."Confidence." *Merriam-Webster Dictionary*, new ed. Merriam-Webster, Inc., 2016.

Chapter 7

Page 107:   One way to explain purpose...Dweck, Carol S. *Mindset: The New Psychology of Success*. Ballantine Books, 2016.

Page 108:   Heidi Grant-Halvorsen, in *Succeed*...Grant-Halvorsen, Heidi. *Succeed: How We Can Reach Our Goals*. Hudson Street Press, 2011.

Page 111:   Philippe decided to put a...Godin, Seth. *Purple Cow: Transform Your Business by Being Remarkable*. Portfolio, 2003.

Chapter 8

Page 114:   Purpose defines the unique gifts...George, Bill. "The Truth about Authentic Leaders." Harvard Business School, 6 July 2016, https://hbswk.hbs.edu/item/the-truth-about-authentic-leaders.

Page 114:   Webster defines authentic as "real..."Authentic." *Merriam-Webster Dictionary*. New ed., 2016.

Page 115:   In the middle of the...George, Bill. *Authentic Leadership: Rediscovering the Secrets to Creating Lasting Value*. Jossey-Bass, 2003.

Chapter 9

Page 128:   We are all fragile when...Brooks, David. "Making Modern Toughness." *New York Times*, 30 August 2016, https://www.nytimes.com/2016/08/30/opinion/making-modern-toughness.html.

Chapter 10

Page 147: **Engaged employees care about their**... "Employee Engagement." Investopedia. 2017, https://www.investopedia.com/terms/p/performance -appraisal.asp-0.

Page 147: **Gallup has published research**... "2017 Trends in Global Employee Engagement." Aon Hewitt, 2017. PDF.

Page 150: **Research by Aon Hewitt suggests**... "2016 Global Purpose Index—Purpose at Work." Imperative and LinkedIn. 2016. PDF.

Chapter 11

Page 159: **Can you imagine a climber**... Excerpt(s) from *The Upside of Stress: Why Stress Is Good for You, and How to Get Good at It* by Kelly McGonigal, copyright © 2015 by Kelly McGonigal, PhD. Used by permission of Avery, an imprint of Penguin Publishing Group, a division of Penguin Random House LLC. All rights reserved.

Page 165: **Imagine if you were asked**... Baumeister, Roy F., Kathleen D. Vohs, Jennifer L. Aaker, and Emily Garbinsky. "Some Key Differences Between a Happy Life and a Meaningful Life." *Journal of Positive Psychology* 8, no. 6 (2013): 505–516.

Page 165: **In a 10-year study of**... Hill, Patrick L., and Nicholas A. Turiano. "Purpose in Life as a Predictor of Mortality Across Adulthood." *Psychological Science*, no. 25 (2014): 1482–1486.

Page 165: **Gallup researchers polled more than**... *State of the Global Workplace: Employee Engagement Insights for Business Leaders Worldwide.* Gallup (2013), 12. Reprinted with the permission of Copyright Clearance Center, on behalf of Gallup.

Page 168: **All stress responses are the**... "Stress Effects on the Body." American Psychological Association. http://www.apa.org/helpcenter /stress-body.aspx.

Page 175: **In 1975, Dr. Salvatore Maddi**... Maddi, Salvatore R. "The Story of Hardiness: Twenty Years of Theorizing, Research, and Practice." *Consulting Psychology Journal: Practice and Research* 54, no. 3 (2002): 173–185.

Chapter 12

Page 179: **Strengthen and increase our admiration**... Wheat, Colonel Clayton E. "West Point Cadet Prayer."

Page 184: **Eighty percent of the people**... UNHCR-Women. January 30, 2018. http://www.unhcr.org/en-us/women.html.

Page 187: **They were approximately 100 meters**... "Colonel Everett Spain, HBS Doctoral Student, to Receive Army Soldier's Medal." Harvard Law

Armed Forces Association, 15 April 2014, https://orgs.law.harvard.edu/armed/tag/everett-spain/.

Page 187: **In the medical tent, he**...Tate, Bernard. "Boston Marathon Hero Awarded Soldier's Medal." The United States Army, 28 April 2014, www.army.mil/article/124781.

Page 188: **First, I'm no hero**...Spain, Everett S. P., Colonel, U.S. Army. Soldier's Medal Ceremony Comments, 18 April 2014, Harvard Business School, Boston, MA.

Page 190: **Philosopher Daniel Putman offers descriptions**...Putman, Daniel. "Philosophical Roots of the Concept of Courage." *The Psychology of Courage: Modern Research on an Ancient Virtue.* Edited by Cynthia L. S. Pury and Shane J. Lopez. American Psychological Association, 2010.

Chapter 13

Page 195: **This is the true joy**...Shaw, George Bernard. *Man and Superman.* Archibald Constable, 1903.

Page 196: **Or, as Viktor Frankl, whose**...Frankl, Victor. *Man's Search for Meaning.* 1959. Beacon Press, 2006.

Page 196: **For example, economist Andrew Oswald**...Senior, Jennifer. "All Joy and No Fun: Why Parents Hate Parenting." *New York Magazine* (4 July 2010), http://nymag.com/news/features/67024/.

Page 196: **In her article "All Joy and No Fun,"**...Senior, Jennifer. *All Joy and No Fun: The Paradox of Modern Parenting.* New York: HarperCollins, 2014.

Page 205: **A research paper from Stanford**...Baumeister, Roy F., Kathleen D. Vohs, Jennifer L. Aaker, Emily Garbinsky. "Some Key Differences Between a Happy Life and a Meaningful Life." *The Journal of Positive Psychology* 8, no. 6 (2013): 505–516.

Page 206: **According to Aristotle, there are**...Aristotle. *The Eudemian Ethics.* Translated by Anthony Kenny. Oxford University Press, 2011.

Page 206: **We can find a good**...From *Grit: The Power of Passion and Perseverance by Angela Duckworth.* Copyright © 2016 by Angela Duckworth. Reprinted with the permission of Scribner, a division of Simon & Schuster, Inc. All rights reserved.

Chapter 14

Page 210: **BILL MOYERS: Unlike the classical**...Campbell, Joseph. Interview by Bill Moyer. Episode 1: *Joseph Campbell and the Power of Myth*— "The Hero's Adventure." 21 June 1988, http://billmoyers.com/content/ep-1-joseph-campbell-and-the-power-of-myth-the-hero%E2%80%99s-adventure-audio/.

Page 215: **According to a Wharton Business**...Mogilner, Cassie, Zoë Chance, and Michael I. Norton. "Giving Time Gives You Time." *Psychological Science* 23, no. 10 (2012): 1233–1238.

Page 216: **Catherine Bailey, with whom**...Bailey, Catherine, and Adrian Maden. "What Makes Work Meaningful—or Meaningless." *Sloan Management Review* (1 June 2016).

Page 217: **Monica Worline is an organizational**...Worline, Monica, James E. Dutton. Awakening Compassion at Work: The Quiet Power That Elevates People and Organizations. Berrett-Koehler Publishers, 2017.

Page 218: **I shared her story of**..."Private Sector." World Food Programme, http://www1.wfp.org/index.php/node/280.

Chapter 15

Page 228: **When you're surrounded by people**...Schultz, Howard. Interview by Carmine Gallo. "What Starbucks CEO Howard Schultz Taught Me about Communication and Success." *Forbes*, 19 December 2013, https://www.forbes.com/sites/carminegallo/2013/12/19/what-starbucks-ceo-howard-schultz-taught-me-about-communication-and-success/#18c57e4428af.

Page 229: **People think I'm the founder**...Schultz, Howard. Interview by Oprah Winfrey. "Super Soul Sunday—The Coffee Culture Howard Schultz Wanted to Bring to America." Season 4, Episode 435, 8 December 2013, http://www.oprah.com/own-super-soul-sunday/the-coffee-culture-howard-schultz-wanted-to-bring-to-america-video.

Page 230: **To inspire and nurture the**..."Our Mission." Starbucks Corporation, 7 December 2017, https://www.starbucks.com/about-us/company-information/mission-statement.

Page 231: **Grow! Grow! Grow!**...Schultz, Howard. *Onward: How Starbucks Fought for Its Life without Losing Its Soul.* Rodale, 2011.

Page 232: **We had lost sight of**...Schultz, Howard. Commencement address to the class of 2017, 8 May 2017, Arizona State University.

Page 234: **Everyone has grabbed onto the**...Stengel, Jim. *Grow: How Ideals Power Growth and Profit at the World's Greatest Companies.* Random House, 2011.

Page 234: **In 1994, the research of**...Collins, Jim, Jerry I. Porras. "Building Your Company's Vision." *Harvard Business Review* (September–October 1996).

Page 235: **A Deloitte study demonstrated that**..."The Purpose-Driven Professional: Harnessing the Power of Corporate Social Impact for Talent Development." Deloitte University Press, 2015.

Page 243: *Forbes* even featured CEO Piyush...Baskin, Jonathan Salem. "Can DBS Make Banking Joyful?" *Forbes* (21 December 2015).

Page 244: Jostein's test came when the..."NPR's Delicious Dish: Schweddy Balls," *Saturday Night Live*, NBC, Season 24, 1998.

Chapter 16

Page 247: It is not the critic...Roosevelt, Theodore. "Citizenship in a Republic." Delivered at the Sorbonne, in Paris, France, 23 April 1910.

Page 247: I would like to end...Brown, Brené. *Daring Greatly: How the Courage to Be Vulnerable Transforms the Way We Live, Love, Parent, and Lead*. Penguin Putnam, 2012. Excerpt(s) from *Daring Greatly: How the Courage to Be Vulnerable Transforms the Way We Live, Love, Parent, and Lead* by Brené Brown, copyright © 2012 by Brené Brown. Used by permission of Gotham Books, an imprint of Penguin Publishing Group, a division of Penguin Random House LLC. All rights reserved.

Page 260: We increase integrity by constantly...Quinn, Robert E. *Building the Bridge as You Walk on It: A Guide for Leading Change*. Jossey-Bass Books, 2004.

Page 260: Research by Anders Ericsson reinforces...Ericsson, Anders K., R. Krampe, and C. Tesch-Römer. "The Role of Deliberate Practice in the Acquisition of Expert Performance." *Psychological Review* 100, no. 3 (1993): 363–406.

Page 263: Angela Duckworth believes this...Duckworth, Angela. *Grit: The Power of Passion and Perseverance*. Kindle edition. Scribner, 2016.

Page 264: When we lead from our...Csikszentmihalyi, Mihaly. *Flow: The Psychology of Optimal Experience*. Harper & Row, 1990.

ACKNOWLEDGMENTS

What I most need to thank for getting this book done is my purpose. Purpose made me choose the hard right over the easy wrong. I put up every possible roadblock and my purpose didn't flinch. Purpose was knocking on my door to write this book and wouldn't stop until I opened up and invited it in. I actually have felt more at home when writing this book than I have felt doing anything else for a long time. That's strange, because in the past writing has been a "have to" as opposed to a "want to"; now it's a "love to" place, and I owe that 100 percent to my purpose.

I have not spent my life writing. And I love well-written books in which each page makes you want to turn it to see what is on the other side. Therefore, I went looking for the elusive ghost writer. I discovered Perry McIntosh, who, with many years at Harvard Business School Publishing and helping others write business books, said yes. Her purpose is "Poke it and see what happens." I feel she has been the most wonderful expression of her purpose with me. What sounded okay when I finished it reads fantastically when she has gotten her hands on it.

I want to thank the more than 75 individuals who shared their stories in the interviews, with special thanks going to those of you who endured the iterative editing process to get the stories 100 percent accurate. For those whose adventures are not featured in the book, without you the themes wouldn't exist. Everyone's stories helped us begin to see what couldn't be seen otherwise: the real impact of leading from purpose.

Brené Brown brought her amazing energy to this undertaking when she offered to write the foreword. We all need a fairy godmother, and Brené is as close as I can imagine to what that must feel like. She read the first draft before anyone else saw it and reintroduced me to Jennifer Rudolph Walsh, who became my book agent. It turns out that Jennifer did a program with me 10 years ago wherein she discovered her purpose. I almost fell off my chair when we reconnected, and Jennifer reached out across the phone line and said, "The world is going to get purpose; let's make it so."

Jodi Scarbrough and Tom Dubinski are the team that made sure what I was saying was actually true and that we referred to leaders, authors, and data accurately and cited them correctly. More importantly, Tom accomplished the detailed and tedious task of obtaining all the permissions, which was almost as much work as writing the book! Jodi, in addition, was the magic elf who kept us all on track and made sure hundreds of details got checked off our list.

I am deeply grateful to Scott Snook for being the ultimate cheerleader who got me into this mess and for insisting that we coauthor the *Harvard Business Review* article "From Purpose to Impact." Writing the *HBR* article made me realize how much more was there to uncover. I tried many times to get Scott to coauthor this book, but he refused. He was wise enough to push me to write this book alone because he knew I needed to fully find my own voice. Thanks, Scott, for kicking my butt as always.

Bill George, my colleague for over 10 years, is front and center in the chapter on authenticity. Our work together and his faith in me have made a huge difference over the years. This book wouldn't exist if not for our collaboration and Bill's support of my stepping more fully into leading from my purpose as a deeper expression of my authentic leadership.

For the last 10 years I have been blessed to have Carol Kauffman as my sparring partner, helping me refine how to coach senior leaders to lead from purpose when everything else is pulling them the other way. Our years of work together have taught me that the deeper truth is always there to be discovered.

Sometimes you need a former brigadier general to knock on your door. Dana Born "forced" me to write an academic paper on organizational purpose with her. Many of the themes in the chapter on organizational purpose are there thanks to her insistence that I share what I had learned after many adventures in making organizational purpose actually work.

Dana, along with courage experts Dina Pozzo and David Hopley, were critical to my understanding the deeper connection between purpose and courage. Dina, at one point your encouragement was what pushed me to uncover what I hadn't been able to see and get it done!

No one knows the journey we have been on to uncover the secrets of purpose better than Amy Avergun, who has codesigned the many programs we have taught over the years. I know a breakthrough is around the corner when Amy says, "Great idea Nick; so what do you think real people would want to actually do?"! The deeper truth comes in many forms and Amy is pointing the way on most occasions.

Another huge contribution to making this book possible is the influence of Jonathan Donner. Jonathan spearheaded a leadership development program for the top 1,500 at Unilever over a six-year period. It was Jonathan's courage and insight that had us bring this work into the Unilever organization. Jonathan actually sat through most of the programs and after each one pushed me to take my game to the next level. Jonathan's purpose is "Cracking big solutions for people I care about," and his "why" is as follows:

I am constantly trying to push through to the other side of things...maybe *solutions* are shorthand for that. I am never comfortable sitting on one side of a problem. I see purpose as a keel on a sailboat—it both keeps the boat from tipping and allows it to move faster. Without it you would slip. It does give you a metaframe...and real direction.

I got the gift of being on the receiving end of Jonathan's purpose, which made me a better man. He also created the idea of asking alumni to return to the program and play a key role as living examples of the impact of purpose. Their contributions, along with many late-night drinks at the bar, became the initial tantalizing insights of the real impact of purpose. To all those who shared a story, I am immensely grateful.

There are a number of the crew I have worked with over the years who on a regular basis made me really step back and think about what I was putting on paper. Kevin Smith, Alph Keogh, and John Haskell have known me for 15-plus years and each comment or suggestion had a way of getting in and the result was the deeper truth on the page.

Jean Capachin brought forth the most fantastic feedback and insights, as someone who hasn't done any of this work but has known me for years. The ability to be kind and direct at the same time is a gift and deserves a big thanks.

To Mauro DiPreta, thanks for magical help as an editor. Yes, many believe all the good editors sailed away and I am here to tell you that at least one has not. One of my greatest desires was to be able to work with a first-class editor, and I got my wish— and you, the reader, got the benefit.

Mom, yes, the one that brought me into this world, was the last person to read and proof the book. Having worked for a printing company for 35 years, you have an eye for what shows up on a page and got to add your unique gift to mine.

Special appreciation goes to my two girls, Renee and Keely, whom I dragged into this adventure over the years and who still love their dad, and to Jeanne, who has been the best partner any writer could ever hope to have. This book would have never had the safe space to be written if she hadn't shown up in my life.

And finally, to the most important person of all: you, for reading this book and actually reading the acknowledgments, which suggests that you enjoyed the journey. A toast to you from me.

INDEX

ABOUT THE AUTHOR

Nick Craig is the president of the Core Leadership Institute, a global firm committed to inspiring people to discover their purpose and equipping them to lead authentically.

Midway through his 25-year leadership consulting and coaching career, Nick recognized that what senior leaders needed most was to access their deeper wisdom in challenging times. The realization refocused his approach to helping them unlock this access, resulting in the Core Leadership Institute's ability to integrate the work of purpose with authentic leadership in the achievement of sustainable business results.

In 2007, Nick began collaborating with Professor Bill George at Harvard Business School; this led them to coauthor *Finding Your True North: A Personal Guide*, which became the course book for the Harvard Business School MBA class Authentic Leadership Development (ALD).

Nick is also the coauthor with Scott Snook of the 2014 *Harvard Business Review* article "From Purpose to Impact" and the *Discover Your True North Fieldbook*.

Through Nick's expertise in the area of leadership purpose, he has worked in partnership with corporate and academic organizations ranging from Ben & Jerry's, Heineken, ING Bank,

LEGO, and Unilever to Wharton's Advanced Management and the United States Military Academy at West Point.

The Harvard Business School case study "Unilever's Paul Polman: Developing Global Leaders" features Nick's work with Unilever. His thought leadership as a Wharton Fellow is documented in Wharton@Work.

You can learn more about Nick and the Core Leadership Institute's work at www.coreleader.com.